'We talk about our longing to see yo[u]
gospel and the church. What we [...]
imagination and perseverance. Beca[...]
people, while they may encounter C[...]
church members. Liz has written an amazing book which
recounts the first ten years of Unlimited through her eyes. She
demonstrates that Christian ministry is not about one person but
many, and that if the work and those involved are not rooted in
Christ the workers will become weary and lose heart and the
work will fail. I commend the book to you.'
*The Right Reverend Dame Sarah Mullally, Bishop of London*

'It's a beautifully written book, full of honesty in the struggles,
integrity in the resolutions and sheer grit to follow God's call! It
encourages you not to be afraid of big vision and inspires you to
go for it and see it through! I'd recommend it for any clergy
couple or those in youth ministry, particularly in pioneering
situations.'
*Louie Thorpe, in ministry (including church planting) for thirty-two
years alongside husband Bishop Ric Thorpe*

'Liz has written a deeply personal account of the realities of
church planting, and any church planter – or any church leader,
for that matter – will resonate with *Beginning Unlimited*. It is raw,
honest, moving and hopeful.'
*Archie and Sam Coates, Senior Leaders, St Peter's, Brighton*

'Liz plays the harp, runs half-marathons, teaches, bakes cakes,
and takes the children to and from school. She is also married to
a vicar, so she moves house, has a succession of students living
with her, prays for strangers, helps young people to believe that
God loves them, and bakes yet more cakes. This diary is
generous and truthful, a compelling account of the small and
large truths of trying to live in obedience to God's call as a clergy
family, negotiating the family's joint vocation as well as the

particular call of each one. Every clergy family should read this book.'
*Jane Williams, Assistant Dean, St Mellitus College*

'This book is about courage – and risk – and challenge – and family – and joys – and struggles – and success – and failure – and vulnerability – and brokenness – and encouragement – and disappointment – and most of all, it's about holding on to God whatever life throws your way. If you've decided to not play life safe, if you've decided to get out of the boat and risk water walking, if you've decided to pioneer with friends and family, this book is for you. Read it… slowly … and let it reality and honesty inspire you in leadership, in life and in faith.'
*Matt Summerfield, Senior Pastor of Zeo Church and former President of Urban Saints*

'This ten-year memoir held my attention so much so that I read it in one sitting. Liz takes us on an adventure through life and time with insight, frankness and clarity. Her voice is refreshingly honest as she brings to life daily experiences, both ordinary and extraordinary.

'This book gave me many cathartic moments, much head nodding and things to ponder concerning the highs and lows of faith, transition, identity and living up to other people's expectations. I laughed out loud thinking about Liz's fancy dress moments. I choked up when she talked about her mother, agreed with her cake-making sentiments and empathised regarding the challenges of church leadership.

'Liz expresses so clearly the journey of seeking God's voice and responding to the challenges we face. I will be giving this book to many people as it has been a long time since I was so enthralled by a memoir and unexpectedly surprised at how much it gave me to reflect on.'
*Minu Chowdhury-Westlake, crisis management consultant and former church planter*

# BEGINNING UNLIMITED

## The Diary of a Church Plant

**Liz Grier**

instant
ap○stle

First published in Great Britain in 2018

Instant Apostle
The Barn
1 Watford House Lane
Watford
Herts
WD17 1BJ

British Library Cataloguing-in-Publication Data

A catalogue record for this book is available from the British Library

This book and all other Instant Apostle books are available from Instant Apostle:

Website: www.instantapostle.com

E-mail: info@instantapostle.com

ISBN 978-1-909728-92-9

Printed in Great Britain

This book is written for James, Josh and Toby. Beginners of Unlimited. May you know no limits.

To my most amazing husband. Thank you for inspiring and encouraging me to write this book. It is our story told with my voice. I love doing life with you.

*'The essence of marriage is that two lives, two whole biographies, are so tied together that they become one history.'*
Robert Spaemann[1]

[1] Robert Spaemann, *Persons: The Difference between 'Someone' and 'Something'* (Oxford Studies in Theological Ethics) (Oxford: Oxford University Press, 2007), p227.

# Author Note

Some names and identifying details have been changed to protect the privacy of individuals.

This is a book of my thoughts, memories and reflections. There is so much more that could be said, and I'm sorry for these omissions. I've done my best to make it tell a truthful story, but I am aware that memories of some events will not be the same for everyone. James has gently corrected me where he could remember otherwise. For the moments where I have made mistakes, forgive me. Memory has its own story to tell.

# Contents

# Foreword

This is a stunning book. I finished it a few moments before beginning to write this. I couldn't put it down. It is searing and yet, at the same time, gently honest. Liz tells her story with insight, elegance, humility and love. It is a story about faith and doubt, about courage and weakness. I found myself rejoicing with Liz in the triumphs and successes, and struggling not to weep over the disappointments and hurts.

Her story deserves to touch many lives because it is so real, so unvarnished, so absolutely how real life really is. Even for Christian leaders. Perhaps especially for Christian leaders. *Beginning Unlimited* tells of the ten-year adventure Liz has been on with her husband, James, and sons, Josh and Toby. They could so easily have chosen the easy option. They could easily have spent the last decade leading a well-established, comfortable church in suburbia. Instead they have poured out their lives to reach young people in and around Exeter who have no church background. They have poured themselves out to build a team that would be more than a team, that would be a family. The Griers are a family that creates family. They can't help it. It is in their DNA.

I have known Liz and James, Josh and Toby for many years, more years than I can remember. They have been an integral part of our summer festivals at Soul Survivor as pastoral coordinators. I have, over the years, loved watching them at work. First of all, it was James and Liz, talking and praying with young people who were often in distress and overwhelmed by their pain. James and Liz have been faithful in their love, patience, kindness and wisdom as they have listened and cared. Latterly I have been moved and thrilled to watch Josh and Toby doing the same thing!

Above all, this is a story of faithfulness in the good days and the tough days. This book should be read by those in leadership, those who aspire to leadership and any who seek to serve Jesus with all their hearts and the whole of their lives.

*Mike Pilavachi*
*Soul Survivor Watford*

# Introduction

I had a pretty unremarkable childhood. Loving parents. Two elder sisters whom I adored and annoyed in equal measure. I worked hard at school. I was both musical and sporty. At the age of eighteen I went to the University of Oxford to read physics. To anyone who knew me I'm sure my life looked both sorted and successful. But on the inside nothing about me matched up to what people saw on the outside. I felt like no one really knew me. I was lonely and wasn't very sure of myself. Up to this point in my life I had kept these feelings in control by achieving. At university, with a whole load of other very clever people around me, that stopped working as a coping mechanism, as a defence. By the end of my first term I had got to the end of the road and the end of my ability to keep on keeping on.

At the same time as I reached this moment of deep self-doubt in my life there was a university mission. Thousands of pounds (for which I'm eternally grateful) were spent arranging events, speakers, seminars and food. Through gentle invitation and my own curiosity I went along, and probably was the most surprised of everyone when at the end of that mission week I decided to follow God wholeheartedly. That one simple decision changed everything for me. The knowledge that I was loved and accepted, exactly as I was, was overwhelming and transforming. To know that I couldn't do anything to make God love me more, that nothing I did would make Him love me less, was liberating. God didn't change me overnight. I didn't suddenly start being fully confident and secure. Even now I still fall into my old bad habits of trying to keep everything in control. But over the years God has always been ready to walk with me when I let Him. The journey that we are on is both the most incredible fun and the hardest thing I could possibly imagine, all rolled into one.

At the start of 2007 I was living in Birmingham with my husband, James, and my two sons, Josh and Toby. More specifically we were living in Harborne, which is like a village within the city. We had been there for five years, we loved the place and the people and were very comfortable both with our friends and with the job. James was associate vicar at St John's Harborne which was a large – by which I mean around 1,000 people – charismatic, evangelical church. There were three services every Sunday, which were relaxed and informal. Life was busy with church, and busy with our two young children. Life was good. I was happy and settled.

But it was all about to change. We knew that James couldn't stay an associate vicar forever, and after two years of looking at jobs, the decision had been made. We were moving to Devon to pioneer a youth church. The thinking was that initially this would take up only half of James' time, so for the other half James would be team vicar across five rural parishes. I had no idea what my part in all of this would be. I knew that we were taking a risk. Stepping out into the unknown. I expected it to be exhausting, exhilarating and faith-building; to demand my all. I did not anticipate that for much of the time it would feel as though we were in a wilderness rather than on a great adventure.

One of the best explanations of time as understood in Scripture I have ever heard came when I was sitting rather uncomfortably on the floor of a huge tent with 10,000 young people listening to Danielle Strickland speaking.[2] In her talk she explained that in the Bible two words are used for time: *chronos* and *kairos*. *Chronos* time is the tick, tick, tick as time passes. It is measured in minutes and hours and seconds. And then there is *kairos* time. *Kairos* is the NOW moment, the moment with God; when time stops ticking and you are right there with God. She went on to compare these biblical times to surfing. At that time I was just learning to surf and I instantly connected with her explanation. I would best be described as an enthusiastic beginner when it comes to surfing. I often struggle out against the waves to find what I think is my optimum position. I then have to wait for an age to catch (or not) a wave. The waiting and waiting, the passage of hours and minutes and seconds, this is the *chronos* time. The *kairos* time is that rare and wonderful moment when gloriously you catch the wave. In surfing I can often spend an hour and count myself lucky to catch one wave. But that one wave, when you have caught it, is worth all the waiting.

---

[2] Main stage talk at Soul Survivor, Week C, Bath and West Showground, 18th–22nd August 2013.

It was a light-bulb moment for me. I realised that when we had set out to pioneer a church I had expected that all our time would be *kairos* time. I had thought that we would find ourselves constantly having moments like the disciples who, after struggling in the wind all night, 'immediately' found that the wind died down when Jesus entered the boat.[3] I thought everything would be 'now' and 'immediately'. We would quickly have a wealth of exciting stories to share and encourage others with. What I discovered, sometimes slowly and painfully, was that for days and months at a time it could feel like we made absolutely no progress. Outwardly it appeared nothing was happening. Of course there were *kairos* moments: exciting, undeniable times when we knew God was with us, and in the planting of Unlimited. But there was also *chronos*. Much more *chronos* between these moments than I had ever anticipated.

Understanding God's view of time – that all the *chronos* is worth it for the *kairos* moment when it comes – came at a period when I was feeling fairly disheartened with church planting, and about our call to begin Unlimited. I was tired. It encouraged and strengthened me to keep going. To keep looking for the *kairos* moments. To keep on believing and trusting God through the *chronos*.

So this is the story of the *chronos* and the *kairos* moments of church planting. The story is told through the journal entries that I made over the years. My journal is not a diary. I don't write in it every day. I tend to turn to my journal when there something I am struggling with, or that I think God is speaking to me about or that I think He wants me

---

[3] Mark 6:47-51.

to remember. It is a record of the big picture, not the minutiae, and I'm sad that many details and events are missing both in the journal and my memory. But the journal entries are honest and vulnerable and I hope they tell the story of how I, as a very ordinary person, struggled and grew within the whole process of planting a church.

# April Fools?

*Sunday 1st April 2007*

We seem to make a habit of moving on April Fool's Day. I don't know whether or not it says something significant about us. An ability to laugh with each other and at ourselves, perhaps not to take life too seriously. I'd like to think so, anyway.

Toby is quite sure that we are not moving. He has the certainty in life that only a two-year-old can have. Despite all the evidence to the contrary, the boxes, the vans, the panic, he calmly announces to one and all that we are not moving. We can't be. The house is stuck. Josh is less sure of anything. His whole world is being uprooted, and he doesn't like change. So he is sticking close to me just in case I disappear into one of the boxes, just like his toys.

The four of us close the much-loved green front door of our house for the last time. Of course I am excited about what lies ahead. But I still need a moment to grieve for what I am leaving behind. This is the house I brought my children home to after they were born. It is where the first

20

steps, the first words were uttered. It has been a house full of friends and laughter and happiness. It has been the place where I felt at home for the first time in my life. It is where the room is where I sat and listened to words that made no sense as my dad told me that my mum was in intensive care and I should get to the hospital as soon as I could. I love that house, and the life that we had lived in it. But after five too short years, we are leaving. The removals men will come tomorrow and empty the house of the boxes. We will be ready and waiting for them when they arrive at our new home.

We crawl our way through the Birmingham traffic for one last time, and nose our way southbound on to the M5. We carry on driving for 140 or so miles until we see the 'Welcome to Devon' sign and know that we have nearly arrived.

## Tuesday 3rd April 2007

I am not meant to be here. Don't get me wrong, I am happy to be here in the country. In fact, we have moved to my ideal holiday home. It feels like it is in the middle of nowhere. We have beautiful views from every window. We are reasonably close to the sea. I'm just not sure I want to live here. We have moved to a village where you can't buy a pint of milk. You can't even walk to buy a pint of milk. The nearest milk is a three-mile round trip, and vastly overpriced at that. How will we ever cope? Hitherto cooking dinner every night involved one if not two trips to the corner shop (which was more of a luxury supermarket than a corner shop, if I'm honest) for a vital but forgotten ingredient. How will we survive in this wilderness?

# Sunday 8th April 2007

'What is this life, if full of care, We have no time to stand and stare?'[4] These lines comes back to me suddenly as I catch the most glorious sunset framed in the patio windows. We've only been here a week, but after years of struggling to remember where the sun rises and sets, it is now ingrained within me. I used to struggle with those questions along the lines of: 'Which way does your garden face?' I never had a clue. In Birmingham we had such a long, thin garden it was pretty hard to make out where the sun was in relation to the terraced houses round about and, even if I could spot it through the trees, houses and clouds, my general knowledge of sun rising and setting did not help me orient the house.

But now I know. It is part of what happens here. The sun rises in the east. Obvious. It starts peering in my small bedroom window in the wee small hours. I can now remember that is the east because the view from my window is of 'Garden Church'. Garden Church is how we refer to the parish church of which James is now vicar. The graveyard is separated from our garden only by three strands of wire. The wire is overgrown with brambles and weeds, and so the church does feel almost as though it is in our garden. Since the first time Josh referred to it as Garden Church the name has stuck. We all call it that now. The sun rises over the east end of the church, suddenly making sense of the fact that pretty much all churches in Britain are located facing east, so that when the sun rises in the

---

[4] W H Davies, 'Leisure', http://www.englishverse.com/poems/leisure (accessed 17th February 2018).

morning it is streaming down on the altar. The sun then tracks around my garden before bowing out in glorious technicolour across the fields that my living room overlooks.

Even though the poem comes back to me twenty or so years after studying it at school, I still can't heed its message. There are boxes everywhere. They have got to be unpacked. I can't sit down until they are. Then, then I will enjoy the sunset.

## Tuesday 10th April 2007

We don't need pictures in this house. In fact anything that we do try to put on the walls is completely overshadowed by the glory that surrounds us. In fact, only one aspect of the house is less than beautiful – a very utilitarian drive. But thankfully the architect of our modern vicarage put no windows on that side, so I don't need to look at that more than is necessary for coming in and out of the house.

It is a complete contrast to our house in Birmingham where our windows on the world overlooked a road, used for a cut-through between major routes, a garden wall and my conservatory whose main function was for drying washing. But I'll continue with the job. The pictures have got to go somewhere and the garage is looking rather full.

## Sunday 15th April 2007

Real life has started, but not quite. What I mean is that real life has started for James. He has started at work. He left the house this morning with that stomach-wrenching mixture of nerves and excitement, when your new job is just a blank sheet of paper, your colleagues are but imaginary faces and your diary is empty. But real life has not started for me. For one thing I'm living in a house that doesn't quite feel like home. It is far too tidy. For another, I don't know anyone here. At all. There is no one I can chat to and, until school starts next week and I can stand outside the school hoping that someone will talk to me, that is not going to change. So we went to the beach. I was determinedly cheerful and we had a great time. As the boys played in the sand I texted friends in Birmingham. Trying to pretend that they should be jealous of me because I was gazing out across the sea kidding myself that I could catch glimpses of the Isle of Wight. Trying not to mind my rather disappointing instant cappuccino bought from the beach café. Definitely not thinking about the deep leather sofas of our local coffee shop. Or thinking about how you make that choice between latte, mocha or cappuccino depending on the night you have just had, and the day stretching ahead of you. Time spent there when we had bared our souls. Or when we just went there to escape the four walls of our houses. Oh yes, I was definitely not thinking about all those things.

And so I smiled. Laughed with my children. Ached for my friends. And theirs. And we enjoyed our time on the beach.

# Garden Church

## Sunday 22nd April 2007

We sat in the front row of Garden Church. We were confined to an uncomfortable pew and for the first time in my life I felt on show as the vicar's wife. The vicar's wife who was desperately trying to interest her children in an unfamiliar service. The vicar's wife who was also bridging the gap to an unfamiliar husband and dad. His robes set him apart from us, and the strange words and constant page-turning of Common Worship and hymns all added to the unsettling feeling of disconnectedness. I think the most positive thing I can say was that it was mercifully quick. After the service was over we said polite 'hellos' to the people around us, but conversation was stilted and the children were hungry and as there was no sign of food we left as soon as was politely possible. We emerged from the chilly church into the spring sunshine and picked our way through primroses and gravestones to our own personal, private gate that leads from church to garden. When I checked the clock I was surprised to be back in our kitchen in time for elevenses, or 'proper lemonsies' as Josh calls it. ('Proper lemonsies' being a promise learned from a cherished godmother. It translates as, 'Let me please finish this task and then we will sit down together and eat a snack and I promise you will have my full attention.')

Instead of the cake, coffee and friendly chatter that I was used to after a church service, the three of us sat alone in the kitchen and I tried to give my children my full attention. I didn't entirely succeed. We were all feeling strange and out of sorts and nothing I could do or say could cover up the fact that we were missing our friends, our church. So we sat and ate our lemonsies and from our kitchen table soon began to watch the people of the parish leave church. I felt awkward and exposed. The kitchen window was surprisingly close to the church path. I was very aware that if we could see them then presumably they could also see us. I wondered what they thought about us. This young, noisy family. I was most struck by how promptly everyone seemed to leave. They didn't linger as we are used to. Their fellowship is brief. They all seem eager to return home, to get on with the rest of the day.

It was so different from what we had left behind. So different from what Sundays used to feel like. What we used to do. I know that any move combines sadness for what has been left behind and excitement at what lies ahead. But this morning the excitement felt a very long way away. You see, despite the fact that we now live in a vicarage with its very own church at the bottom of the garden, and the fact that I have just been to a service where my husband was undeniably the parish vicar, this is not what we came to Devon to do. It is not a job we had ever imagined doing in any of our youthful dreaming about what life would be. It is true that I have always had a hankering to live in a village, but never in our married life had James let me entertain such an idea. His reasoning has been persuasive and fair. He recognises that we like the hustle and bustle of a city. We love big churches, where congregations of 500 are normal. We like modern worship music. We even enjoy drums.

So about 100 times this morning I asked myself what on earth I was doing with my family in a church of no more than twenty people? With the music for hymns being played on a CD player, and a twenty-year gap to the age of the person closest to mine? In a church that challenged my narrow definitions of church and faith? Where I didn't know if I would ever belong? All I could see this morning was that there was no one else at my age and stage. It felt lonely, and I wondered if we had made the right decision.

Instead of dwelling on these thoughts, I need to remind myself why we are here. We have come to Exeter to start a youth church. I will choose to rejoice that in this time where there is real pressure to reduce clergy numbers, with a constant struggle to make diocesan finances add up, the diocese has stepped out in faith to do something new and bold. They have created half a post for a vicar to start a youth church. On paper it was quite a unique role. Half the time working in Exeter city centre with a focus on sixteen to eighteen-year-olds. Half the time working across five rural parishes. An incongruous mismatch of pioneering fresh expression and traditional Common Worship. In fact, it was such an unlikely mismatch no one else even applied. We wouldn't have considered the job for a moment but for a chance God meeting involving diarrhoea and vomiting. James was told about the job while working as pastoral coordinator at the Soul Survivor festivals in the summer of 2006. [5] There had been an outbreak of diarrhoea and vomiting in the camping area for those from Devon and he was sent in to provide support. From the briefest of encounters and a sketchy outline of what the job may entail we knew that it was what we were called to do. Even with my mixed feelings of this morning I still know that we are called to the whole package. The traditional and the new. But today the traditional feels too much for me, and I can't help being more excited about the new.

I can't get too excited, though, as currently there is no church and there are no youth.

## Monday 23rd April 2007

Someone swore in front of me today. Actually blasphemed. Funnily enough, the swearing itself did not bother me, as there was actually swearing in Birmingham too… But I was bothered by the reaction. It was school pick-up time and there was the usual banter among the parents. Well, I presume it was usual, but as I know nothing and no one here, I can't be sure. And then someone swore. It was as if the group froze, and from behind me a dad said 'mind your p's and q's – the vicar's wife is here.' That made me pause

---

[5] Soul Survivor is a charity that puts on a range of events for young people, for youth leaders and for the whole church, to help people deepen their relationship with Jesus. In particular, each summer there are many Soul Survivor camping events, each of which last five days. For more information see www.soulsurvivor.com.

for thought. I am not used to being defined by my husband's role. I'm not used to people behaving differently around me. In Birmingham it was subtly different. At the school gate I was known as Liz whose husband was a vicar. Here I am going to be known as the vicar's wife, with all the expectations that the role brings with it. I hope I'm up for this.

## Saturday 12th May 2007

I woke this morning with a real sense of anticipation. Today is Soul Exeter. A little mini Soul Survivor celebration in Devon. Not only do we get to go every month, but even better, we get to be part of it! Finally something that should feel familiar, like a comfy pair of slippers. I felt like I could breathe a little more deeply today. As a family we have attended the Soul Survivor summer camps in Shepton Mallet every year. We love the people, the worship, the overwhelming sense of the presence of God. We even love the camping. So to be able to have this every month seems too good to be true. I honestly couldn't wait!

Later as I stood in a dusty church hall, knowing no one and feeling desperately awkward, I was disappointed to count fewer than fifty youth. We had been told around 300 young people would attend, so this didn't quite match up to my expectations. It didn't feel very much like Soul Survivor either. It felt like the celebration had lost its party overtones and it was now just going through the motions.

I thought back to the vision and extraordinary generosity that had started Soul Exeter. Five years previously, two local vicars, but more importantly dads, had approached Mike Pilavachi and asked if he could help their children. Every year their children went to Soul Survivor and came back with a fresh excitement and passion for their faith. Hopelessly the dads then watched this ebb away through the year, praying there would still be enough left to get them to Soul Survivor the following year. At a chance meeting with Mike, they desperately asked him if anything could be done. I doubt they had much hope and yet Mike said that if they could gather 300 young people, he would send people down to lead a celebration each month for a year. Although this was an amazing offer, they knew they could never get 300 youth together, and with great regret had to refuse. Mike offered to do it for 200. Again, they said there was no way. In the end, Mike asked what they could manage. They said thirty (I think that was probably their children and friends and faith for a few more). Mike agreed! For more than a year, Soul Survivor sent a worship band and top-class speaker from Watford to Exeter – a dispiriting four-hour drive on a good day, and I am sure many trips were not good. The team from Watford would lead Soul Exeter and then drive through the night to be back in time to lead worship at their own church first thing in the morning. It can't have been easy. In that year of sacrifice, something really special began. From a starting point of thirty youth, they regularly began to attract around 300 young people.

However, right now, that all seems a long time ago. Five years on the celebration is still going but it feels tired and despondent. The two trailblazing dads'/vicars' children had grown up and only one is still around. The dads continue to sacrifice one Saturday every month to this event. They have started something amazing. But now it is our turn to take up the baton.

## Thursday 31st May 2007

I miss my mum. She would have been sixty-five today. Grief is a funny thing. It sneaks up on you unawares and punches you in the stomach and reminds you forcefully, painfully of all you have lost. Some days you know that it is going to come and visit. Today is her birthday and always will be, with or without her, so you prepare yourself to try to lessen the blow. Other days you are completely unprepared and you are flattened by the pain all over again. My children have had a loving granny stolen from them. It is as though their childhood has been robbed of something special, and the unfairness of it all never seems to ease.

It saddens me that I have no deep, deep assurance that she is in heaven. I hope with all my heart that she is. I think she believed in God but had been alienated by church. She had been deeply hurt by what she felt was rejection when she didn't measure up to her church's standards, and so had turned her back on religion. I hope in the end that her belief in God was enough. Sadly, I have many conservative evangelical friends who have told me forcefully that merely believing in God isn't enough. Many didn't realise as they were propounding their point how personal their comments were. To them they were arguing in the abstract. Where I painfully wasn't. But I'm starting to hope that God is infinitely more generous in His mercy and grace than I have previously assumed. I don't think I'm becoming liberal and woolly in my thinking. I still absolutely believe in the Bible being the Word of God, and that we must hold fast and faithfully to that. But I am learning that God is infinitely more generous than I am. Infinitely more loving. Infinitely more forgiving. That being a Christian, living this life with Him, takes on many shapes and guises. One size does not fit all.

And it is since we have broken out of our large charismatic church into the depths of rural Devon that this change of thinking has started. We knew as we accepted the job that we were called to the whole package of James' job. The traditional and the new. Even if ultimately we would end up pioneering a new church, the parish role was never just a stopgap. But I also knew that the traditional would be really personally challenging. I had spent much of my childhood singing in church choirs but had not discovered a living faith until I went to university. In my naïvety I thought everyone who chose to worship in small village churches were like I had been: enjoying the tradition, the music, the liturgy, but completely missing the point. I did not expect to find God at work. Or people of faith. And I was so wrong. The people I have met here were nothing like I expected. It is true that I would not choose to worship in the same way. But that gives me no right to judge the validity of their worship. It is genuine and heartfelt and wonderfully different to mine. And I'm beginning to love that fact. I would have pigeonholed them as having a faith that is dried up and out of touch with God. But on getting to know them better I have learned that they are joyfully serving their loving Saviour in a place that I would find too hard to contemplate. They don't always find it easy, but do so because that is the calling on their life, and are doing it in joyous communion with God. Living here forces me to the conclusion that the definition of 'Christian' is far broader than I had previously imagined.

It is with delightful irony I realise I too have been pigeonholed by other Christians in exactly the same way. To say that your husband is a team vicar across five parishes brackets you into an antiquated stereotype of baking and the Women's Institute. It's not me at all, although I am rather fond of baking. The church that I attend says nothing of my heart for God. How I love Him, long to know Him better, love hearing His voice. More, I hope it speaks of my commitment to His calling on my life; that I will be obedient to Him, even if it takes me out of my comfort zone and pigeonholes me somewhere I would, if I'm honest, much rather not be. I was truly comfortable in my large Anglican charismatic church. The worship connected with my heart and soul, the sermons were challenging and relevant, and hardly ever over the thirty minutes' time limit (honest!). The people were lovely, easy people to be friends with, and city life suited me. Its anonymity and friendliness all mixed up together felt comfortable. But I know now that there is a great danger that we judge people solely on the church that they attend, and not by their heart for and knowledge of God. I am wiser and better for learning that.

# Vicar's Wife

## Monday 2nd July 2007

I was told this morning that I looked like a vicar's wife. I do not take it as a compliment. It's not fair that I feel this way because I know some fabulous vicar's wives I would be proud to be compared to. But I'm guessing today that somehow I'm conforming to some stereotype that is not altogether flattering. Make mental note not to wear that skirt again.

## Thursday 5th July 2007

It is hard not to get overwhelmed with the enormity of what we have come to do. We have come to start a youth church with no other adults, no building and no youth. We are just one family living eight miles away from where this new church is going to start. I am a worrier. I know that, and I also know that it is a pointless activity. As I spiral into worry I need to remind myself of the quotation from Corrie ten Boom – 'Worry does not empty tomorrow of its sorrow, it empties today of its strength.'[6] I also need to hold on to the promise that God made us when we were contemplating the task we were being called to. James and I called together a group of people whom we loved and trusted, to pray, at a time when the job felt way too much for us. A wonderful man told us not to worry about building the church. That was God's job. God would find the stones to build the church. We just had to polish them. Then they would become living stones and be the church. But this was going to happen one stone at a time. So today I take my eyes off the worry of 'youth church' and all that could and should mean, and focus on waiting for God to find the stones, and make sure that I'm ready to start polishing.

## Saturday 21st July 2007

I have moved from a community where I smiled at the hairdresser – had to start dashing past her shop when we changed our allegiances – knew the greengrocer and the newsagent, where the coffee shop knew my husband's order before he spoke it. And yet all these people didn't really know us. They knew our faces. We were part of their fabric. Occasionally in crisis they contacted us, but in the main we were all anonymous to one another. We could dip in and out of society as we chose. We could pretend to ourselves that we were there for everyone, but in reality had only space for so many friends. We were friendly with everyone but not everyone was our friend.

---

[6] https://www.bibleinoneyear.org/bioy/commentary/2186 (accessed 19th March 2018).

It is not the same in the village. We are not anonymous. Everything we do has an effect. So today I find myself covered in green face-paint, wearing a green ball gown and a long red wig. I don't do fancy dress. Ever. I think it comes from a fear of being laughed at, not with. An insecurity in myself that really doesn't want to be the centre of attention. So I'm not sure why I ever agreed to dress as Princess Fiona from *Shrek*, and to spend the whole day dressed that way in front of my new potential friends. And also in front of people who already don't like the vicar, or his wife. I've been saddened to find that there are people here who, although we've never spoken to them, don't like us. They don't know us, but they know that they don't like the church. And therefore by extension they don't like us. We've heard some of their reasons. Vicars not visiting in times of sickness, weddings refused, not available for funerals, always being asked for money for the roof. It wasn't us, but they have taken it personally. So now I am aware that our actions too will reflect on the church. And ultimately therefore on to God. I don't really want to give them any more ammunition.

But I'm not being totally honest when I say I don't know why I am doing this. I know that I agreed because James is very persuasive. He loves people, he loves fun, he loves getting stuck in, being helpful. Being around him can be a bit like being around the party. Everywhere he goes people engage, laugh, trust and reveal themselves. Today is the village Fun Day, and James has persuaded us to join him at the centre of it. We've only been here two months but have got stuck in to represent the church at this village fundraising event.

The day is fine and bright. All our fears for a washout are unrealised. A wonderful, exhausting day is had by all. The cake stall serves hundreds of cream teas, the stands all do a brisk trade, we enjoy watching the police dogs in the central ring. I revel in this new community, where everyone knows everyone, where we all matter to each other, to a greater or lesser degree. It seems that all my private worries for ridicule and hostility have been unfounded.

## Saturday 18th August 2007

It is good to be home. It has been wonderful to spend five days camping in Shepton Mallet for the Soul Survivor festival, but it feels utterly luxurious to be tucked up in bed after a good long soak in the bath. I also feel more secure, more settled about what lies ahead, and what my part in it should be. I'm called to be a mother to the young people that God brings to us, to fulfil a role that is missing in many of their lives. When I think about it, it is just an extension of what I already do. What I love doing. And I know that I can do this thing that we have been called to. God has prepared a place for me, it fits me. I just need to trust in Him.

## Wednesday 29th August 2007

James has been invited to a barbecue! Possibly not the most unusual event in an average summer, but this invitation has come totally out of the blue. Somehow God has engineered this meeting and it seems really hopeful. A group of young people and their parents want to talk to us about youth church. Many of the churches in Exeter know why the Church of England in Devon have employed James, but so far no one has really wanted to talk to him about youth church. In the main he has been greeted by deep suspicion and mistrust. There's a genuine fear that our plan is to steal all the youth from surrounding churches to create some cool and trendy all-singing, all-dancing youth celebration. It has been hard to get past that misapprehension to really talk about our vision, to say that we have really come for the unchurched youth, for those with no knowledge or contact with church. James told me that only 1 per cent of youth are currently connected with church in Devon.[7] We are told that, at best, if a church manages to connect with all the young people it has any affiliation with, that would still leave 75 per cent[8] of young people who have absolutely no contact with anyone in a church. They literally know no one who could invite them along to church. Our heart is for the 75 per cent, but we need help. We need workers. We have so far failed to find any. But maybe this barbecue is the start of God providing.

---

[7] Based on Exeter Diocese Mission statistics compiled from church attendance in 2006.

[8] This 75 per cent statistic came from an informal discussion with the Fresh Expression team at a Soul Survivor Festival in the summer of 2007.

# Letting Go

*Saturday 1st September 2007*

We are not renewing our TV licence. I think I'm in shock that we have finally made such a momentous decision. Well, it seems momentous to me, because at the end of the day what I do is collapse on the sofa and watch the TV. I'd like to be more wholesome. Truly I would. To read a book. To listen to classical music. But all my life it has been the same, even when I'm frantically busy. I honestly did not think I would ever change. But life in rural Devon has changed this. Despite buying a large super-duper widescreen TV, of the type that only a bloke can truly get excited by, we still have no Freeview or even Channel 5. That combined with the fact that we need to get the aerial repaired, as what signal we do have is rather intermittent, particularly when it is windy (which is often), means that we have taken the plunge. We have tried to convince the licensing people that we no longer require their services, which is harder than you might imagine. We have disconnected all our aerial wires and have absolutely no means of receiving a signal, but are on three-month probation. A funky little TV van could pull up at any minute and accuse me of watching TV. And I need to be able to prove to them that I'm not and, more importantly, that I can't. If this does happen, it will invariably happen when James is out, and I live in terror of the licensing people arriving. I can barely turn the set on now, it is so high-tech. I have not got a chance of proving to them that I am without signal. I can only hope that James has indeed disabled the system, and that the TV is not so clever as to have an internal aerial or something lurking that will prove me to be a liar.

## Wednesday 5th September 2007

The children have adapted to their morning routine. We are finding it much harder. It formerly involved a tired parent shepherding them downstairs and pressing the 'on' button. Now said parent has to be awake enough to negotiate the choice of DVD. This involves correctly remembering whose day it is to choose. Which is never easy when you are half-asleep. If for any reason the parent can't remember they can face the gauntlet of trying to choose a DVD collaboratively or let the children determine for themselves who decides. Both alternatives are fraught with problems. Josh's and Toby's choices of DVD on any given day are never the same. Both will feel passionate about their preference. Or you can let them decide whose turn it is to choose. Sometimes they agree on this. Not always. But they will always fiercely defend what they believe to be fair. It is certainly true that the day starts much more calmly when only one child is awake at the time the decision is made.

Instead of instantly turning to the television, once or twice the children have invited me to play with them. They have quickly learned that I am not a morning person. I can hardly focus for about half an hour after waking, let alone hold a conversation, or play. Although I am delighted for them to be playing happily rather than watching TV, I am completely unable to join in.

## Monday 10th September 2007

I miss work. When people ask 'What do you do?' I miss having that easy conversation-starter by which you are happy to define yourself. I love staying at home with my children but I don't love people's reactions when I tell them that this is what I do. So often it is a conversation-killer. Frequently there is an instant assumption that I have nothing to talk about other than nappies and baking, combined with a response that is a patronisingly enthusiastic reaction affirming my life choices. Which I wasn't aware I needed. The only hope for a normal conversation relies on me either changing the subject completely, asking them about their work or telling them about the job that I used to do.

But I also miss having purpose. Achieving. We were told we could have it all. Girls of my generation were sold this lie. You can have a fantastic career, handsome husband, wonderful home. You can do it all. Perhaps I was naïve and sheltered in my girls' day school, with my mum who was always there for us, picking us up from school, watching our sports fixtures, enduring our endless concerts. I never questioned whether or not she was happy with her lot. I just assumed that I would have more. I would do all that she did. Be gloriously there for my children, and be famously influential as well. Well why not? Margaret Thatcher was prime minister of the UK, Indira Gandhi was prime minister of India, the Queen was, well, Queen. Women were ruling the world and I was going to be one of them.

Before I had Joshua I was working for a Research Council funding science and engineering research projects in the UK. I travelled the length and breadth of the UK, enjoying the first-class travel and the swish hotels and meals that accompanied the job. We moved to Birmingham when I was seven months pregnant, and the timing meant it was the perfect moment to start my maternity leave.

At that point I still thought I was going to have it all. A fabulous career and a wonderfully compliant baby, who would grow into a model child, and I would miraculously be there at all the right moments. That of course went hand in hand with the ideals that we soon-to-be-parents held. Ideals that are not uncommon in many couples in those blissful last few months of your first pregnancy. You are waiting for everything to change, but reality is still far, far away. You say to each other smugly that this baby isn't going to change your life, merely enhance it. Nothing material has to change about your life. You can still go out to dinners, concerts, camping, climbing. Whatever. The baby will just have to fit in. You are so proud of yourselves that you are not going to become like the XXes who since having their baby sometimes refuse dinner invitations, and have had to stop attending evening church. Oh no, you proudly think, 'We will not be like that!'

But that was not my reality. Joshua just didn't seem to have got that memo. He was not compliant. He did not sleep when the books said he should. He did not eat when I wanted. I was used to being in charge, in control. I was successful and respected. He knew none of that. It was my undoing, and yet also my beginning. Becoming a mother shook me to the very core. I could no longer find value and self-worth in what I did, because I felt like a complete failure a lot of the time. Slowly and with infinite patience, God drew me to Himself. Motherhood was nothing like I expected. My relationship with James had been radically altered from a fun partnership to an endless round of chores and responsibilities. We were exhausted pretty much the whole time. My relationship with God also felt totally different. I no longer had the extended quiet times. Now I struggled to read the Bible and pray. If I had a rare quiet moment, I was more likely to fall asleep than achieve something spiritual. But to my surprise God wasn't disappointed in that. He wasn't disappointed in me. He met me even in my briefest readings of the Bible. He spoke through friends and wise people around me. I found myself connecting in new, deeper ways with the songs at church. I found that even if I only heard a portion of each sermon, each time there was something God wanted me to hear. God drew me close with words and verses and encouragement and gradually I started to find my worth in being a child of God. I learned that God knew my every thought. He knew me inside and outside. He knew all the bits about me I'd rather no one ever knew. And yet He loved me. Completely and totally. I was accepted, forgiven and loved. I learned afresh that I did not need to do anything to be loved by Him. That nothing was expected from me. And that knowledge was transformational.

So motherhood was not an easy journey, but I knew beyond doubt that it was the best thing that had ever happened to me, and I was in no way ready to return to work when my maternity leave ended. Joshua was nine months old when I had to return from my first period of maternity leave. I say 'had to' but that isn't totally true. I didn't have to. I did have a choice. I chose to because otherwise I would have had to return my maternity pay. But wrenching myself away from my home, my baby and my friends was far harder than I had anticipated. It was not made any easier now that work was a two-hour drive away from home. Before moving to Birmingham, getting to work involved a one-hour train journey. It was something I enjoyed. It gave me time to read the Bible, reflect and pray, and on good days (or perhaps bad ones) involved the treat of a takeaway cappuccino. Now we lived in Birmingham city centre and my work was still based in Swindon. My job had been changed and modified at my request to be more suitable for a working mother. It was reduced to part-time hours and was much more office-based. Sadly, now the commute was not a relaxing train journey, but a frustrating drive across Birmingham city centre, a slog down the M5 and then another hour of frustratingly slow cross-country lanes until I reached Swindon. All the time I was checking the clock, trying not to be late for work. Trying not to be late home for the childminder. Trying to get everything done. To be there for everyone who wanted a piece of me.

And those were the good days. On the days when I did not have to commute, my employers had set me up with a home office. Everything I could possibly want. Laptop, internet, phone, mobile. Everything but people. I would sit in my office for seven and a half hours a day, willing the phone to ring. Waiting for something to make being at work more bearable.

Before this time I had always thought myself a bit of a loner. Very happy in my own company. Quite sure, actually, that I really could be an island. Yes, I liked people and friends, but very much on my terms and in my time. Having children changed all that. I was now desperate for company. Someone to share the ups and downs with. Someone who would just distract me from the day-to-day, would have fun with me and take my mind on to topics other than when the next feed was due, the next clean nappy. Now I had friends I could see more than once a week, and didn't seem to get tired of me. I could pop round to their house uninvited and be welcomed into their life without them making any special effort for me. I and my child were just welcome to sit and be with them.

This was a completely new idea for me. In my childhood it was a rare event for people to come and visit. Of course, there were friends. But they were never mine. I was the youngest of three children, the youngest of the cousins, the youngest of the children living on our street. My sisters' friends came round, and they visited in return. Sometimes I was allowed to tag along. But not often. So I got used to being alone, and was very happy with that. It came as a bit of a shock when I married James that he did not agree with this at all. He was not going to sit at home gazing into my eyes or, more truthfully, watching television. We were going to have fun! And so we did; we had dinner parties and games evenings. The weekend wasn't the weekend without at least one dinner at our house. The best weekends were when we were invited out as well. And I loved it. I loved feeling a part of these people, and inviting them round, and them actually saying yes. I never quite got over the surprise that people wanted to spend time with us, but deep down I know I put it down to the fact that people wanted to spend time with James (and quite honestly, who wouldn't?) and they sort of had to put up with me.

But since having children it was quite different. I had friends of my own. Friends who quite liked James but came to dinner with us because of me! Friends who could cope with seeing me more than once a week. In fact, who seemed to want to see me more than once a week, and didn't mind if my house was in a state. Who would come and eat toast rather than my best Jamie Oliver recipe, just because we were doing life together. And I was missing all of this. Sitting in my little home office, up in the eaves of our house, I would wonder what they were all doing today. Were they at someone's house or had they gone to the botanical gardens to enjoy the unseasonably warm weather? Possibly the last good day for a while? Perhaps they had gone shopping or to the latest soft play area. Perhaps they were talking about me. Missing me too. Or perhaps not. Maybe I had wafted through their lives. A pleasant interlude, but not much lamented in its passing.

So returning to work after Joshua was born was not a success. Probably I was the most surprised that it didn't all work out fabulously. And although I was not expecting it, I quickly realised that being a working mother just didn't fit with me; I joyfully and gladly gave it up and became a mother of (eventually) two small sons. And it was easy in Birmingham. I had a structure of friends and playgroups, activities and places to escape to. There was never any need to feel alone or overwhelmed with motherhood. I don't feel quite the same now. There is no church toddler group bursting with noise and energy and love to go to, to be looked after for a precious two hours, to connect with other people who are similarly feeling tired and happy, beyond themselves yet contented. Unless I want to start it, there never will be. We can't walk anywhere from the village. There aren't even footpaths to explore. Everything is a car trip. Everything seems much harder work. Everyone is friendly, yet no one is my friend. As I drop Joshua off in his classroom and watch him happily find his place at his table, I desperately hope for someone to stop and talk to me. But it is not to be. I head out from school, clutching Toby's hand, and as we cross over the humpback bridge that leads to the vicarage, we start to make plans for another day. I'm lonely. I miss the easy camaraderie of work.

# Small Beginnings

*Tuesday 11th September 2007*

I am utterly shattered. From the moment I picked Josh up from school it felt like we were on a countdown. Everything had to run with military precision, so that at 8pm we were ready when the doorbell rang. (Note to self – next week we leave door open so that the doorbell doesn't disturb the children. Eight times.) Because tonight was the night. Tonight we started youth church! Well, OK, not quite. Tonight we met with eight young people who were disillusioned with church, and were keen to explore with us what youth church might look like. James had already met them at the barbecue during the summer, at which they decided to start meeting with us in our house to talk further. But they had never met me. Honestly, I was terrified. What would they think of me, of us? Would they simply be too cool to even look me in the eye? Would I spend the evening feeling like the geeky kid in the corner that no one wants to talk to? Would we have anything in common? Why on earth would they want to spend their evening with us?

But from the minute they arrived, none of that seemed to matter. We were just a group of people keen to work with God to reach the young people of Exeter. The age gap disappeared. The young people want to reach out to their friends. We are almost old enough to be their parents. But it didn't matter. We found as a group we had the same heart to reach out to the lost and lonely. None of us had the answer, or a clear idea of what the next step should be. But we knew we were the building blocks. The first stones for this church. We are going to meet every fortnight. For want of a better name we will call the group 'Tuesday'.

Next week I will make more cake. They seem very hungry.

## Friday 14th September 2007

Have joined DVD rental company. After two weeks of cold turkey from TV, I think we can make this work. But I do need something. So I have decided I am going to watch all those series that have hitherto passed me by. All the series about which my friends exclaim, 'I can't believe you haven't seen it!' Will throw in a couple of period dramas for low evenings.

## Tuesday 25th September 2007

A fortnight has passed. It is Tuesday again. I was not as nervous tonight. I have tried to rationalise with myself that as they were returning to our house for a second evening, we can't have been all that bad, all that hopeless or completely out of touch. Tonight we started praying with them. Despite their longing to reach out to their friends, they themselves have a hopelessly muddled picture of God and church. They can't separate where church ends and God begins. Where church has hurt them, and some of their stories are heartbreaking, this has merged into their view of God. He has become for some a harsh and strict disciplinarian. Our passion for these youth, which remains our passion for everyone we meet, old or young, is that they will learn how God sees them. How He has created them. What is unique about them. We believe that if they know who they are and how very loved they are, they will spend less time looking at others and comparing themselves unfavourably, and more time doing the stuff that God is calling them to do. Living their life to the full. Doing the stuff that only they can do. Idealistically and maybe hopelessly optimistically we imagine a church with everyone serving in roles that fit them uniquely. We want to see people released to be the very best version of themselves rather than people just trying to fill the gaps, which is often painful and unfulfilling for everyone.

The only way for them to know how God sees them is to ask Him. We sit there with our Bibles and hearts open, and let Him speak. Each person in that room is special, and we will rush over no one. My heart sinks as I realise it will take us months to pray for each one of them if we meet only every fortnight. Yet that is what we commit to do. We are going to polish these stones.

Tonight we prayed for just one guy. It feels very small and yet it is the start.

## Monday 1st October 2007

James is out again tonight. I shouldn't moan. I know I shouldn't. I like my space, and after a full-on day with the children I need some time to do my own thing, without reference to anyone else. But sometimes it would be so marvellous to have more than one night in together in a row. To be able to relax together. As it is, there are so many things that we need to do that we can't easily do when the children are around; an evening in is a chance to 'get on', to 'achieve'. On the rare occasions that we do decide to sit down together and watch a film, then James comes complete with either his filing, or his laptop, and gets on with his admin. Which hardly makes for a romantic (or – let's set my sights lower – companionable) evening.

## Monday 8th October 2007

We have a name. It feels strange. For so long we have referred to 'it' as youth church. It was never catchy, or going to catch on, but we had nothing better. But now we have. We are going to be called 'Unlimited'. We think it sums up all that we hope for in a church. That the church – no, must start calling it by its name – that Unlimited will be able to communicate the unlimited boundlessness of God's love, that nothing is beyond Him, nothing too bad that He can't forgive and restore. It feels good to have something solid, something real to call ourselves. Unlimited. Must remember that name.

## Friday 12th October 2007

The question I dread the most is: 'Have you settled in yet?'
It is always asked sincerely and kindly. But it instantly
alienates me from the community we have just joined. It
jolts me out of kidding myself that I've become part of the
group – one of the girls. It reminds me all over again that
I'm a newcomer. These are not my friends. They probably
will be. But they aren't yet. There is an impassable gap of
time together, life shared which I can pretend isn't there
until someone voices it, makes it tangible and enquires of
me, 'Have you settled in yet?'

## Wednesday 7th November 2007

Today Toby is being Peter Rabbit. He is quite insistent that
he is not feeling very well. Despite having tucked away
blackberries, bread, milk and Tweenies pasta shapes (a
significant deviation from the original, I know – but what
can you do with twenty-first-century children?), he now
wants tucking up in bed with an apple and some
'camouflage' (his words – not quite Beatrix Potter's) tea.

## Tuesday 13th November 2007

I can't help but be concerned. Two of our Tuesday group
have started going out with each other. It seems wonderful
at the moment. They are both lovely and sensible and
committed to the group, and now to each other. But they
are very young. What will happen if they ever split up? The
others in the group might feel they ought to take sides,
which could fracture it irrevocably.

## Monday 3rd December 2007

Anna truly feels like a gift from God. A real answer to prayer. She is someone I can be totally honest with. Who doesn't go to my church, live in my village, share much of my life. She is someone to pray with. We both have in common that we have moved from Birmingham to Devon. That is, in fact, the connection that brings us together. She is the friend of a friend from Birmingham. Anna has chosen to rent a house in a small town about four miles from us, while her house in Birmingham is on the market. At first I am desperate to make her want to buy in my village, to have the complete country idyll, and a ready-made friend to boot. But actually I discover that our separateness is good. That we don't have friends and situations in common means we can be completely honest, and expect honesty in return.

And so tonight we met and talked. We really talked. Well, to be more accurate, I talked. It feels like the end of a drought in many ways. I monopolised the conversation but I just couldn't stop myself. It felt so good to have someone who is listening to me, the real me. The whole of me.

# Four Become Six!

## Thursday 3rd January 2008

Youth church seems one step closer today. On Tuesday nights we are exploring ideas of what a church focused around young people could and should look like. The young people are also growing in their knowledge and love of God, but we are not church. Until today I would have said it consisted of just four of us – two of whom I slightly discount as at present they can get free rail travel, free milk and free entry to many historic houses – but now, today, there are six of us. Not a huge shift, I know, maybe not even enough to have a party. But enough for me to feel the burden lightening just slightly. Now there are four adults who can pray, meet together, encourage one another and try to work with God to bring about this church of His.

I got to know Steve and Helen through a group that met for a year or so in our home in Harborne. We were a group of people who decided to meet together because we felt that our lives and ministry didn't match up to what we saw in Jesus'. We wanted to hear His voice more clearly, we just didn't know how. We weren't living the life we thought the Bible promised. We were not experiencing true freedom. We didn't think our lives looked or felt radically different from our non-Christian neighbours, and we wanted to know why. We were asking questions. Was this all there was? Or were we missing out? As well as knowing them through the group, James also knew them on a deeper level, having ministered with them every week for a year.

We knew God wanted us to ask them to join us in Devon to start a youth church. We just never thought that their answer would be yes. Humanly we assumed that they couldn't, wouldn't, shouldn't leave thirty years of life lived in Birmingham, their family, their jobs and their friends. We didn't know that they had been living with a promise for that entire time that they would move to Exeter. The fact that Steve and Helen have come to join us in this adventure at times overwhelms me and at other times makes me think they're slightly crazy. What are they thinking? Why would they do it? What if we fail and there never is a church, never any more than a few youth in our living room? The responsibility for their decision is not mine, I know. But they have sacrificed so much more than us to be here that it is hard not to worry for them, to want the very best.

## Monday 3rd March 2008

I find that I'm starting to really look forward to Tuesday nights. Completely unexpectedly I find myself loving working with youth. They are so quick to learn, so keen to give it a go. They don't come with all the baggage that adults do. We haven't been doing anything that radical with them. Jesus tells us that He is the shepherd, we are the sheep and that the sheep know His voice.[9] So we are helping them to recognise God's voice in their lives. The starting place for us is looking at who the Bible says God is, and who the Bible says we are. There is nothing new in any of that, but the difference with this group is that I can see before my eyes the difference it makes when they start to believe it. When for the first time they understand that they are a child of God; then not having the best relationship with your earthly parents can be put into some kind of perspective. Or knowing that you are loved, truly loved, exactly as you are. Understanding that God knows you completely and loves you in spite of all that He knows. It is an amazing truth. It stills that constant striving to compare, to compete. I guess I'm particularly enjoying it because it contrasts so starkly with the home group from our last church. It was a similar group with similar teaching. The only difference was in Birmingham the group consisted of adults, not youth. We found that the adults knew the teaching but, for many, life and circumstances had made these truths feel less life-changing, less liberating. This made it much harder and much slower to move on and learn to hear God's voice. Not so with this group. They are eager to learn, eager to try, and also know that it is OK to make mistakes. We don't all get it right all of the time.

---

[9] See John 10.

## Tuesday 6th May 2008

Youth church is such an unhelpful label. We use it out of laziness but it in no way conveys what we think Unlimited, or indeed any church, should look like. Because a church cannot exist of only one generation. Such a gathering would be a congregation or a celebration, but it is not church. To me church exists gloriously of the old and the young, the rich and the poor, the academic, the sporty, the loud, the quiet. A veritable smorgasbord of every walk of life, where we all live and learn together and from each other. A church that tries to consist only of youth would, I think, struggle on every level without the richness that other members would bring. So we must stop using the label 'youth church'. We want to be an all-age church, not a youth church. Even that label makes me think of many family services I have attended that have tried to cater for every age group, and have honestly only been partially successful. Maybe a multigenerational church with a particular mission to youth sums us up better. Much more of a mouthful, but maybe a more helpful label.

## Saturday 10th May 2008

We were warned that there was a different pace of life in Devon. But I don't think we really believed anybody. I mean, how different can people be? It is wrong to stereotype by county. Surely people are people, regardless of where they live. I'm beginning to wonder if I was naïve in not listening to this advice.

Despite my initial disappointment with Soul Exeter, as a family we have really poured ourselves into it. All four of us attend every month. Even James' mum, Sara, travels up from Plymouth to help with the logistics of babysitting, often exiting with two very tired but overexcited boys as the opening worship draws to a close and the speaker steps up. Gradually we have seen things begin to change, improve. Numbers have started going up and up. We changed venue to somewhere more central, with more atmosphere, with less clearing up. And numbers continued to grow. April saw around 200 youth, and I have to admit we sat back proudly at all we had achieved. Patted ourselves on the back and thought 'we must be doing something right'. And then today, May, we are right back to a disappointing fifty.

Apparently it's what happens in Devon. Everyone says so. If you get a sunny day, people go to the beach. Churches are consistently emptier from April until September. There are all sorts of pressures on the youth from exams, to work, to … going to the beach with their mates. You can't fight it, we were told. There is a different pace of life in Devon.

Well, they may be right. That may be what happens. But I am not going to roll over and give in. Where on earth does it say in the Bible that it is OK to give God a miss because it is a nice sunny day and you would rather be on the beach? Rather, we are told not to give up meeting with one another.[10] It may be the pace of life in this place, but it does not mean that I am ever going to accept it or endorse it. I will fight it and continue to place God, and to try to get

---

[10] Hebrews 10:25.

others to place God, over all else in their lives. Yes, even over surfing.

## *Sunday 1st June 2008*

Sometimes I feel so helpless. I watch James juggle an ever-increasing workload, and I know I can't help him. I can only watch and pray as his responsibilities expand beyond the time available. As his study carpet changes slowly from a deep, luxurious red to an avalanche of paper. Some vital. Some destined for recycling. Impossible for anyone but James to know the difference. And the problem is, he is his own worst enemy. He is too nice. No, that word doesn't do him justice at all – he is a genuinely lovely person, and people want to spend time with him. He is also immensely wise. He is the first person I turn to when I have a problem. And the first person many others turn to as well. He likes people, connecting with them, having fun with them, being there for them. But that all has a cost. He can't be everywhere for everyone. But he wants to be. He feels responsible for those around him, those he has committed to be there for.

And that is only a part of the problem. He has other calls on his time as well. The funeral, baptism and wedding visits. The PCC meetings and, of course, team vicar of five churches means lots of PCCs. School governor. It goes on. Everything he does is worthy of his time. But only the family can see how much it takes out of him.

I don't think I'm a good vicar's wife. Or maybe I am. But I have never been one for meekly taking up the slack. For releasing James to go off and do his stuff while we trail along in his wake. Think of me more as a passionate mother tiger, fighting ferociously for her cubs. Fending off the next attack on his time, fighting for his presence, working to remind him that we are more important to him than the next phone call or meeting.

But even as I fight for what I so strongly believe in, I know that I too am part of James' problem. I am another call on his time. In a way, another pressure. Perhaps if I could be more loving and giving, and not so demanding, he would give to us more freely and out of a joyous sense of love rather than duty. Or perhaps we truly would get drowned out in the noise of all the others. I don't know. I will try to be there more for James as well as the children. To place myself alongside him and work together as a team.

But I will never, ever do his filing.

# Doubts and
# Difficulties

## *Wednesday 11th June 2008*

I have a secret. I don't want to tell James. I don't want to
make his job any harder. But put simply, it's this – I just
don't see how there will ever be a youth church. The task
ahead is just too big. We are too small. My faith is too weak.
From whichever angle I look at it, I just can't see it working
out. I begin to wonder if it would be so wrong to just enjoy
the time that we have in this beautiful village while our
children are small and then take our references from our
last church and move on. Ignore the half of the job that
failed. But even the act of committing this thought to
paper, of giving substance to something that was only an
uneasy feeling, draws my thinking to the early Church. I
have been reading through the book of Acts recently and I
was struck by the story in Acts 14 where Paul and Barnabas
appoint church leaders and then pray for them. Not just
nice, comforting prayers that are a bit like a pat on the

head, but earnest, heartfelt prayer. They even fasted (in my opinion, things must be serious if fasting is involved!). Paul and Barnabas knew how those first church leaders felt. Knew that they too were overwhelmed by the task in front of them. Knew that they had to keep their eyes fixed on Jesus, running the race set before them, [11] not getting distracted by the enormity of it all, but simply trusting for each step of the way. Although I wouldn't dream of putting what we are doing, our calling, alongside that of the early Church leaders, the story does remind me of our original commission to this job. We are only called to polish stones. One at a time. God is going to build the church. I know that I will have to be reminded of this again and again over the next few years as the path ahead remains lonely and uncertain, and church growth is painfully slow. But for now, in the stillness of resting with God, I know that I can continue. Anyone can continue polishing one stone at a time.

## Saturday 19th July 2008

How has this happened again? The girl who doesn't like fancy dress has just spent the day dressed as 'a bag for life' in the middle of a field. Fancy dress for me is always awkward, but is especially toe-curlingly embarrassing when no one else really joins in. I have to take pride in the fact that I gave it my all. My talented mother-in-law created four person-sized bags out of hessian for us to wear at the village Fun Day. I'm not sure anyone really understood what we were wearing, or even why, as we were the only

---

[11] See Hebrews 12:1.

members of the committee to embrace the fancy dress theme. But we tried. The boys had fun, and as a family our costumes were certainly memorable!

Unlike last year, we have been fully involved from the beginning of this Fun Day. Planning started with the first tentative meeting of a brand-new committee back in January, and progressed to the glorious day we shared today. Obviously the clue is in the name: the day is about fun, but it is held to raise much-needed funds. For such a small village, fundraising can be difficult. The four main groups in the village are the school parents' association, the village hall, the pre-school and the church. They all need funds, and actively fundraise, but rarely together. When we arrived we found it so strange to attend the bingo in aid of school, the fashion show for pre-school, the disco for the village hall. Many of us had involvements in more than one of these groups, but working together proved painful. Groups were territorial and suspicious. This year, however, the Fun Day committee sought to bring all the groups together for one enormous fundraising extravaganza. And it worked! The community put aside their differences and pulled together for one amazing day. The sun shone, the cream teas sold out. The police dogs didn't show up as they were called out on a proper job, but it didn't matter. James had the time of his life announcing everything over the loudspeaker system. A fun day was had by all.

Sadly, the day did not end well. At the end of the evening we were sitting on a hay bale enjoying the sunset when we became aware of a commotion at the gate. James went over to investigate. Unfortunately he was too slow, and a small fracas had escalated to a full-blown police incident. Some teenage boys were trying to gain entry, but as they had been drinking could not be admitted because of the licensing laws. It was a small thing but it was like lighting a touchpaper between the people involved. We were surprised it got out of hand so quickly. We had had no knowledge of the feuding that existed between several families in the village. It seems that the pain and anger are still as raw as ever. The police were needed to calm everyone down. It was a very sorry end to what had been a great day.

## Sunday 20th July 2008

James has just been threatened because of his involvement in last night's affray. It seems such an overreaction to an alcohol-fuelled incident.

## Tuesday 22nd July 2008

The situation from the Fun Day does not seem to be getting any better, and we are so keen not to be at odds with anyone. James has been advised that talking about things will make things worse. But we can't believe that is true. There must be a way to reconcile, surely?

## Sunday 3rd August 2008

I'm thinking that choosing James' birthday to be totally honest about how I'm really feeling probably wasn't very good timing. And it is such a shame because we had had such a lovely day that I still can't quite believe that I ruined the evening. The day had been wonderful. I love birthdays. I delight in making a fuss of the people that I love. I like to plan every moment of the day. Everything we eat is special. Everything we do is thought about. I really enjoy playing games. Because every Grier birthday, be it adult or child, includes birthday games. They are very simple but afford us much fun. First apple-bobbing so that faces get nice and wet. Then the knife-and-fork game where a chocolate perches perilously on a beautifully sculpted cake of flour. The challenge is to make one cut to slice away some flour, but for the chocolate to remain securely on top. The person who causes the chocolate to topple then has to pick out the chocolate using only their mouth. Obviously my tactic in the game is not to be the person who causes the chocolate to fall. Because if the chocolate falls during your go, you have to face part two. I try to avoid a face full of flour at any cost, so make minute cuts into the flour, well away from the chocolate. The boys, however, have a completely opposing strategy and slice away dangerously large amounts of flour every time it is their turn, willing the chocolate to fall. There is always great suspense as the chocolate teeters on the top. When it has finally toppled the person who attempts to retrieve the chocolate has to remember that as you approach the flour mound you absolutely must not giggle. If you can avoid breathing, even better. If you fail at all at this, you are instantly surrounded by fluffy white clouds of flour that stick like glue to your wet face. Further digging around in the flour for the chocolate only adds to the flour makeover that you receive. Everyone is giggling by the end and I love the simple fun of it. It is a silly game. But brings us much joy as a family.

So after what was a pretty wonderful day, when the boys were finally tucked up in bed and the last trek up the stairs had been completed to provide water/cuddles/teddy, why then did I decide to bare my soul? I honestly started just trying to make light conversation. Despite being weary after the long day of jollity, I did not want to end it in front of a DVD. I was desperate for some grown-up, uninterrupted conversation. But so rare are these moments for us it was only a short while before it all came out. My despondency about youth church, my utter loneliness and longing for Christian friends. My yearning for families that we could spend time with.

It wasn't the most heartening of conversations. We both know there are no solutions, no quick fixes to where we find ourselves. But just the simple act of talking about it, sharing it, has made me feel differently. I know that as we go through today we are walking together. James knows how I feel and what I'm going through. He can't make it any better. But he lets me know, in many small ways, that I am not alone, and that I am not unnoticed.

Today in the quietness that follows the excitement of the birthday, that feeling of let-down when you have another whole year to wait until everyone makes a fuss again, I remember a prayer that was said over us as we left Birmingham. That prayer spoke of a desert, and of our time in Devon being like a barren wilderness. I remember feeling at the time that it was not an image I particularly relished, but also knew that being new anywhere, losing all that feels familiar, can feel like a wilderness. So I understood that probably the picture was accurate. What I totally failed to comprehend, however, was the timing. In my mind the desert would last for a maximum of six months, and then would come the desert rains. Water would fall on the barren land and wonderful, amazing, lush plants would start to grow where before there had been just dry dust.[12] I knew and loved the image of flowers rejoicing and blossoming in the wilderness from reading Isaiah. It was only now that I was beginning to connect this picture with another part of Isaiah, where we are told that God's thoughts are not our thoughts, neither are our ways His ways.[13] So where I had been thinking six months or so of wilderness, never had God said that that was what He was thinking. I had so much to learn about trusting and walking with God. But thankfully God is patient with us, and gives us many chances to grow with Him, and He is not in the desperate rush that we are.

---

[12] Isaiah 35:1.
[13] Isaiah 55:8.

# The Rough and the Smooth

## Wednesday 3rd September 2008

James met with the bishop to discuss his ever-increasing workload, and to share with him the vision for the next year. He returned from the meeting hugely encouraged, loved and affirmed. He felt listened to and more certain that he was doing the right thing at the right time and at the right speed. I am glad that he feels that way. I hope I will feel that way soon. But I don't at the moment. I am just disappointed that nothing has changed and his workload remains the same. A dear friend summarised the meeting for me as leaving James in 'a disappointing continuance of an untenable situation'. Sums it up perfectly.

## Tuesday 16th September 2008

James is grappling with the sovereignty of God at the moment, which therefore, as so often, means that this is the subject that the vicar's wife is grappling with too. Little one-liners are thrown out over the dinner table such as, 'Why does God allow suffering?', that get us debating issues. I'm not sure it helps me, it can often leave me with more questions than answers, but James is an external processor. Which means he talks a lot to find out what he is really thinking. The whole discussion during dinner clarifies the issue for James. This is not true for me. I take longer to work things out. I need to go away to think, to read, to find our more. I bring up the rearguard.

I wonder if it takes me longer because I am a scientist at heart. I would like to see the world in black and white. Grey makes me feel uncomfortable. If the world was, for example, black, white and pewter I might learn to adjust and cope with it, but when we come across issues and people who remind me that the world is actually a myriad of shades of grey, then I struggle and it takes me longer to find my way through than it does James. For him it is just obvious.

## Wednesday 17th September 2008

James is being blanked at school by individuals involved in the Fun Day incident. In the corridor people turn around and walk in the opposite direction when they see him coming. We are beginning to understand why feuds live on in small communities if these are the after-effects of such a small incident. There is certainly no sign of reconciliation yet.

## Monday 13th October 2008

Another evening spent with Anna. I am better behaved now. Whether it is because we meet up regularly, or I'm just more conscious of it, we both get to talk. I no longer monopolise the conversation like a woman who has been stranded on a desert island for months, starved of companionship. But, tonight, perhaps the fact that Anna was up ten times last night with her daughter (yes, really, ten times: it was one of those nights that was so bad that the only thing that keeps you going through it is counting the intrusions into your sleep – or lack of it) meant that I ensured that I listened to her more, talked less and made sure she got home in reasonable time.

## Friday 17th October 2008

It's Friday night and I'm too excited to go to sleep. It's not helped by the fact that I'm sleeping in a rickety, creaky bunk bed. But I'm not awake because I still have the childish love of bunk beds that Josh and Toby do, but because it is our very first church weekend away. We have taken our wonderful group of eight young people to a beautiful cottage on Dartmoor which comes complete with wood-burning stove inside and burbling brooks and granite tors outside as far as the eye can see. It is a chance for us to have time and space as a whole group to determine the next step for Unlimited. We have been praying with these young people for just a little more than a year and we can see them blossoming in the knowledge of who they are and how loved they are, and we feel sure that this weekend will be the start of the next chapter for our church.

## Saturday 18th October 2008

Dartmoor seems a little less idyllic today. I didn't sleep well in my bunk bed, and lack of sleep never brings out the best in me. I'm in charge of food and I'm not enjoying the kitchen. You can't have both gas rings on full, and a mouse found its way into our cereal store overnight. The city girl in me shudders at the very thought. There is also no phone signal. Ordinarily that would make me very happy. The thought of a weekend away from the constant demands of a phone would delight me. But not today. Josh and Toby are staying with Grandma; the plan is for them all to join us tomorrow for Sunday lunch. But Josh has tonsillitis. He feels terrible. He wants his mum. I feel terrible. I want to be with him. I am torn between family and church, and not for the first time. So between every session I run up the tor to catch a faint signal to check how he is doing. Apparently I miss James doing exactly the same, and Sara patiently fields alternate phone calls from us all day. With every call she tells us not to worry and to focus on where we are, what we are doing. I tried. But it isn't easy.

## Sunday 19th October 2008

We are home, our family reunited. It has been good and hard in equal measure. The cost for our family was high and yet I think it was worth it. This morning we started looking at what church is and should be and I was so excited to realise that in the young people in that little cottage on Dartmoor we have it all. In one we have a pastor: her love and compassion for people flows out into everything that she does. In another we have a worship leader, who as his heart chases after God can take us with him. In Chris we have a prophet, a man who can hear so clearly from God for himself and for others and with an ability to communicate it too. We have practical gifts in design, in PA, in baking. We have all that we need. God has brought a church to us, as He promised He would. In the young people we have all that we need to be a church. We still need a building.

## Tuesday 18th November 2008

We have a new member of church! It is early days but I have such hope. The most exciting part is that she is not a youth. Well, not really. Jess is a first-year student reading sports science at the University of Exeter who heard James speaking, liked what she heard and has come to find out more. She is only nineteen but she wants to get stuck in with our vision of reaching the young people of Exeter. The fact that someone else can hear what we are about, grasp it and want to get involved lifts my spirits more than I could have imagined. It makes what we are doing simultaneously feel more grounded and more exciting. It gives me new strength to carry on.

# The End of the Beginning

*Tuesday 23rd December 2008*

I ought to be delighted. I ought to see the bigger picture. I know that we are not here to build our own little empire. That God's plans are bigger than mine. I know His thoughts are not my thoughts and His ways are not my ways. I know. But all I feel is emptiness. The excitement that I felt after the weekend away has gone completely. Our tight-knit group has evaporated.

For fifteen months we have been teaching, praying, pastoring our little group of youth. Our genesis of youth church. We have been gently showing them who God is, and separating that knowledge from seeing what church is. They have learned that a church is made up of people. People who may well hurt and harm you. Sometimes unintentionally. Sadly, not always. But that church is the very best gift that God has given us. It is a place where we belong. We need each other. We need church. We have taught them all of that, and most of them have caught our passion for church and have one by one gone off to find themselves churches. Places where they can belong and serve and grow. They found themselves as impatient as I am for Unlimited to become something real and tangible. But unlike me they have not had the patience to wait. They have gone and found places where the Church is now. They have found places where they fit, are welcomed and accepted. Where they feel at home. Two of the group left because their relationship broke up; it caused an irreparable fracture, as I feared. One decided the cost of Christian faith was too much. For him it would have meant changing and facing up to things, and he was just not willing. So for various reasons all eight young people have left. Jess, Steve, Helen, James, myself and the boys are all that remain. We will have to start again.

I should be pleased that they have all joined other wonderful churches. I want to be able to say job done. One day I will say it and mean it. But not today.

## Monday 5th January 2009

I've done this before. It wasn't easy the first time. Sending Josh in his unfamiliar and slightly too large uniform into a classroom of strangers. At least that time I had Toby to distract me, to demand my attention. To take me out of myself. This time after leaving Toby for his first day at school I just have the empty house. And the cleaning.

As Rockbeare is such a small school the classes are combined, which means that big brother Josh is in the same class. There to protect, help and guide Toby (I fondly hope) as he starts school. Toby, of course, is delighted. Not in the least bit bothered. It has been his deepest wish for a very long time to join his big brother and many of his friends who started school in the September intake. To him it is just a big adventure with a uniform that he loves. It is just me left worrying, wondering how he is, how he is getting along. Hoping that he is being included. Feeling loved. Having fun.

But I can't afford too much time to worry, as I have my own work to get on with. Totally out of nowhere I have got myself a job. I wasn't looking or even thinking of returning to work this quickly, but somehow I find myself about to start teaching maths at the University of Exeter. It is only for two days a week, and only for two terms initially, but I am excited to be using my brain again, seeing if I can remember all that I knew at some point in the past, and more importantly if I can communicate it to a class full of students. I think it is the classroom element that scares me most. I love teaching people who want to learn, who listen and question, who engage and challenge. I am not at all sure that I have the skills to control a class if they are bored, disengaged or rowdy. I fear I may be shrill or shouty, and, either way, be totally ineffective. Still, I can't dwell on that now – lessons to prepare.

## Wednesday 14th January 2009

Today was the first day of my new job and I tentatively think I might survive. The groups that I have to teach were lovely: kind, courteous and polite. They seemed to understand what I was teaching. Such a relief. I hadn't realised I had been quite so tense until this evening and I felt properly relaxed for the first time in a long while.

## Tuesday 20th January 2009

Jess has brought her friend Ruth to Tuesday nights. Another sports scientist. She seems keen, but terribly busy. I'm not sure she will find time for us.

# Life Beyond the Family

*Thursday 22nd January 2009*

I went out tonight. Left the children with James and just went. It felt so lovely to be the one going out, leaving bedtime and the dishes to someone else. Almost like a night off. I'm not sure that James is very impressed. Since we have had children we have kind of had an unspoken arrangement that I won't make fixed plans for a weeknight in case he has a meeting that he needs to be at. It sort of makes sense, but I found myself resenting his evening meetings. I started becoming more and more aware of the things that his job stopped me doing. I knew it wasn't healthy and that I had to do something to stop it sowing a bitterness within me that would only ever be destructive.

So I have been fairly radical. I have joined an orchestra. As well as making sense to me, it may resolve another source of tension in our house. For the whole of our married life we have had a battle in our dining room.

James' prized possession is the antique table that he inherited from his grandmother. James knew he wanted to be a vicar from his early teens, and his grandmother seemingly has been promising him this table, as it 'would be perfect in a vicarage', pretty much since the time he made this decision. The problem is that it is antique. Yes, it is a thing of great beauty, but it is also massive. It is built for a house that is of utterly different proportions to the modern vicarage we currently find ourselves living in. The table by itself would be absolutely fine in the dining room, but there are two of us in this marriage. When I promised all that I have I would share with him, James knew he was getting a part share in a keyboard, a flute, assorted other instruments but, perhaps most significantly, also a harp. All of which, and their associated music, take up space. In this house we have to slither around between table and sideboard, between keyboard and chairs, between harp and bureau. There is simply not enough room for all our possessions to be comfortable, and to make it worse, I hardly play the harp any more. Most of my music-playing is now within church and the harp has only been used in recent years at Christmas. It seems like a huge sacrifice of space just to play 'Silent Night' once a year. So I've decided it is make or break time. As much as I haven't fully thought through the implications of what this means, I think the time has come to use it or lose it. To start finding time to play the harp, or to reluctantly sell it to make way for family life.

So tonight I set out by myself to an orchestra rehearsal in the middle of Exeter. I've never moved the harp without James' help before. I had to ask a tuba player to help me move it in, and then I had a kind of live audition in front of what I later discovered to be an orchestra composed mainly of professional musicians. It was terrifying and exhilarating. I loved it. I wasn't perfect, but I was better than I expected to be, considering I haven't seriously practised in fifteen years. I'm hooked back into the world of classical music and James will just have to refuse Thursday night meetings, as they are going to be my night!

## Thursday 26th February 2009

I love the fact that God speaks our language. It doesn't matter who we are, from professor to toddler, He has the words to connect with us. We spent this morning praying with Lucy. Things in life had knocked her confidence and she was being robbed of living fully as the person that God had made her to be. Circumstances had told her that she was unlovable and didn't matter, and that is what she now believed. The belief that you are unlovable leads you to act accordingly and so it was a vicious cycle. When we looked at Lucy as God saw her we saw a smiling, laughing person who should light up a room. Who loved people, connecting with them, drawing them in, giving value and love to everyone. But Lucy often wasn't that person in a group. She was quiet and withdrawn. She avoided attention and would deflect away from herself in the mistaken belief that she had nothing to offer and was worthless.

So we started praying with her this morning. It is not going to be a quick fix, to untangle these thought patterns that she has lived with for so long. However, God longs for her to be free, and so this morning we made a start. Before she left we wanted her to go with an image of something tangible. A picture of how God saw her. In her head she knew that God loved her. She knew various Bible verses quoting this fact. She earnestly believed them for other people. But she did not, could not, believe them for herself. She could not make head knowledge into heart knowledge. In her mind there was nothing special about her. So we asked God to give her a picture, to speak straight to her heart. We waited in the quietness and almost instantly she started smiling. We continued to quietly pray for her without interrupting or getting in the way. Afterwards she told us that she had seen a shop window full of cupcakes. All sorts of wonderful, beautiful, enticing cupcakes. Instantly this had her attention as she loved cakes and baking. As she was drawn into the window, to look more deeply at the display, one cupcake in particular caught her eye. Right in the centre of the window was the most fabulous cupcake she had ever seen. All the cupcakes looked good, but this one stood out from the others. This one was special. According to God this cupcake represented her. And in that picture God spoke straight into her heart. He took the Bible knowledge that she had and translated it into her heart. She knew that she was special. She was unique. She left the room smiling. I am still smiling now, knowing that God speaks the language of cupcakes.

## Tuesday 10th March 2009

Another student, Alison, has joined the church. Ruth has also decided to make time for us. Alison has joined because she has heard that we go out and talk and pray with young people on the Cathedral Green and that sounds exciting to her and she wants to get involved. At once I'm both delighted and perplexed. I know it sounds exciting, but there is an equal measure of terror that goes with it. At least, there is for me. So far I have not been able to join the groups. It is always arranged on an ad hoc basis, more often than not in the afternoons when I am picking up the boys from school. A part of me is relieved I haven't been free. Perhaps she is bolder than me.

It feels right and healthy. Jess, Ruth and Alison joining us. It feels like a new team is being raised up. A team passionate about reaching unchurched youth.

## Monday 16th March 2009

Sometimes it feels as if all I say is 'no'. 'No' to the boys who are constantly pushing the boundaries. 'No' to James who is always fighting to fit more into the diary. James and I have often joked that one of the reasons we got married was so that he would remember to eat meals, would be forced to stop. But I'm not laughing at the moment. I seem to constantly have to rein him in. To tell him gently that he can't meet the needs of everyone. I'm not enjoying it. I understand the way he feels absolutely pulled in two. There is always a good reason why someone needs to see him, and why they can't wait. When we take a minute to step into their shoes, to understand their journey, we are filled with compassion and we want to help. The result is that we, us, the family, our marriage gets squeezed out of the edges. In my role as a tigress, fighting to protect my family, my cubs, I get it wrong, I know I do. When I am overwhelmed by everything, without meaning to I drift away from God and take the protection into my own hands. I shelter the boys from James' work, because I have never wanted them to feel the burden of ministry and our calling to Devon. But I know this is dangerous too. I am teaching them to be selfish, to put themselves first. I want them to know that the Christian life is about pouring yourselves out for others and for God. That we need to have servant hearts. There is a balance. I so want to get it right. But it is exhausting.

I feel I'm saying 'no' a lot at the moment. I hope that I'm getting the balance right. I don't enjoy it.

## Saturday 2nd May 2009

Tonight we are eating pasta. Much pasta. Because, and I can't quite believe this is true, and it is certainly a sentence that would have had me laughing in disbelief not so long ago, but (deep breath and drum roll) tomorrow I am running the Exeter Half Marathon – 13.2 miles. I will be running every one of them.

Anyone who knew me from my school days would find this sentence as ridiculous as I do. Sure, I enjoyed sport. But I enjoyed food too. I was slightly larger than most of my peers and therefore slightly slower in the sporting department. 'A very solid B team player' would have summed me up beautifully. And I absolutely avoided running at all costs. I didn't seem to mind it in the context of sport, when there was a reason for it. But running by itself? No, thank you. Whenever it was suggested to me, I would laughingly deprecate my physique and point out all the reasons why I just wasn't built for running. But in the few months when we were preparing to come to Devon, something in me changed. Something stopped me refusing offers to go out running, and in the end I accepted, and went out one cold dark November evening for my first-ever run with Jane.

It should have been absolutely fascinating, running around Harborne after dark, being able to see into the hearts of so many homes. Some were eating dinner; others, lounging in front of the TV; other homes were deserted. I knew that James would have loved it, but I was totally overwhelmed with the burning sensation in my lungs and legs. The slow uphill of Wentworth Road that was never-ending and the gentle patience of Jane encouraging me and talking to me and doing everything she could to keep me going and get me round. I have no idea how far that first run was. I fear it was incredibly short. I was more than delighted to return home, and, despite a long soak in the bath, struggled with the stairs for days afterwards. 'Ow, ow, ow' announced my arrival long before I actually made it into the room. But I was determined to continue. It seemed important. I had bought the kit.

By the time we moved, I could run – well, shuffle is probably more accurate – for three miles without stopping. I had found in running a way to escape, to breathe, to find space and perspective. It helped me sleep better, and let me eat cake once in a while. I was hooked.

I had thought that running was going to be important in Devon. I knew I would miss running with Jane. I had no idea of the impact that it was going to have on my life. Tomorrow I will be running a half-marathon. Something I thought I could never do. But much more importantly than the running is the fact that I will not be running alone. I will be running with Sarah, who over the last eighteen months has become the most precious friend to me. Sarah is taller (her legs are endless) and faster than me – yet for reasons that I can't quite understand, doesn't want to run the half-marathon at her much faster pace. She doesn't want to run alone.

It was she who, when we both realised that we had run the same route that morning approximately twenty minutes apart from each other, suggested that we should run together. I was beyond nervous when she picked me up for that first run. It was one thing running with Jane, who was a very good friend, slightly shorter than me and knew I had never run before in my life. But to run with Sarah was another thing entirely! As it turned out, it was absolutely fine. Yes, Sarah had to slow down to let me keep up, but she genuinely seemed to enjoy the company, and for her the sacrifice was worth it.

From that first run we have never looked back. We have run together four times a week, often before the children are awake. Sometimes on icy, ungritted roads with head torches (what were we thinking?), and for every mile that we have run, we have talked. Not for us the chasing after faster times and better PBs.[14] Running is about friendship, about sharing life together. And we've found that in three hours of uninterrupted chat every week you can do a lot of life together. She has become my closest friend, knows more about me probably than James (as we do not have three hours of uninterrupted chat in a week), and tomorrow we will do the challenge that I suggested six months ago. Half-jokingly, I suggested that we should give

---

[14] PBs: personal bests.

ourselves something to aim for, and have to admit to being more than a little shocked when she agreed, providing I sorted out the training schedule. So I did my best, and off we went. Tomorrow we will see if I got it right.

## Sunday 3rd May 2009

Tonight I am tired but so, so happy. I doubt I will be able to move tomorrow. But for now that is not important. We did it! It was the toughest thing I have ever attempted. Especially the hills. So many hills. And then, of course, Pinhoe Road. Pinhoe Road is long and steep, and in the Exeter half-marathon runners have to go up and down it four times along the route. It is awful. It doesn't feel too bad at first. It even appears to start with a bit of a party. At the bottom of the hill is a church that would ordinarily be having its Sunday morning service. But on half-marathon day the congregation comes out of their building on to the pavement. The joyful sound of their worship band greets the runners as they commence the climb and the lift to the spirit is indescribable. But it is not enough. The boost to my morale didn't get me all the way. I didn't notice until afterwards that at every hill Sarah had deliberately started telling me a story that both was interesting and required no input from me. I now know she did it deliberately. It was so kind. It definitely helped keep me going.

Running was not something in my comfort zone. Yet today I think I have proved to myself that you can do almost anything if you set your mind to it. You don't have to be defined with labels from your past. These are all things that God has been teaching me over many years, but today I have seen them physically manifested.

## Thursday 7th May 2009

We've got quite used to the fact of James being blanked at school. People ignoring him, turning around and walking the other way. Half of me wants to laugh as it seems so comical in the school corridor of this tiny school of only sixty pupils. James used to laugh inwardly at each occurrence. But nothing changes and it is no longer funny; James uses it as a prompt to pray. Who else notices these scenes every morning we will never know. I'm half-grateful that the reactions are not more violent. But it's not comical. It is just so sad.

## Monday 11th May 2009

I've been asked to renew my contract with the university. Not just continue as I am, but to increase my classes and schedule to the equivalent of four school-length days. It has put me in something of a dilemma. I have always liked certainty and safety, knowing what I do. Being in control is one way of looking at it. Being sensible and responsible could be another. I always envied people who knew they wanted to be a doctor or a nurse. Just knew what they were called to. I imagined that from the moment they knew what they were going to 'be', then their life became straightforward, the path before them was set and all they had to do was walk along it. I tried as a teenager to want to be a doctor. It didn't work. Even then I couldn't fool myself that I would be any good with all the blood and illness. But I have retained a vaguely jealous antipathy for those who do know what they want to do. Here before me is a great opportunity. It uses my skills, it plays to my strengths, I even enjoyed it. The sensible answer is 'yes'. But it just isn't sitting easily with me. At the moment we spend every Monday morning meeting with Steve and Helen. Praying for Unlimited. For the young people. For the four of us. For all that we are called to be. I could not sustain this meeting and a job and also care for my young family. To give up money, status and position for the sake of a prayer meeting, for a church that barely exists, and maybe never will, goes against all my worldly instincts, my upbringing. I am in a dilemma. I won't take the job at the university. But I'm worried that I'm making a foolish decision.

## Friday 26th June 2009

This evening Exeter Cathedral was filled with 1,200 young people. They filled the main body of the cathedral, raced down the side aisles and spilled out on to the Green outside. They got to see the cathedral as never before. Before the massive West doors was a skate park, inside there were bands, prayers spaces, nail bars, game stations. Outside in the cloisters was every kind of inflatable imaginable. The evening sun shone and it was a happy event. James had been asked to organise a youth celebration as part of the diocese celebrating being 1,100 years old, and, although I haven't been involved in much of the planning, tonight I got to play too. It was amazing. The evening stands in contrast to the more formal celebrations that are planned for the rest of the weekend. I don't think in all its years the cathedral had seen anything quite like it, and yet I hope the legacy will live on. Twelve hundred young people saw that the church, not just the building but the people too, are not necessarily the stereotype they have written us off to be. They had fun. We had fun. God's name was glorified in a unique way in His house today.

## Saturday 18th July 2009

Another year. Another Fun Day. But it has not been fun. Trying to get the groups to work together has caused pain and upset, deep suspicion and anger. This year we dressed as scarecrows but my heart was not in it. Probably all the visitors came and had a marvellous fun-filled day. I hope they did. I don't know that I can face it another year. Perhaps we need a break. Some fresh perspective. The day ended with yet another fracas, involving village rivalries, alcohol and violence. A heady mixture.

## Monday 20th July 2009

Once more, James has attempted to meet and resolve this year's Fun Day incident. Again he was met with a blank refusal to talk, or to seek restoration. When I think about the situation I just feel so sad. It seems like such an exhausting way to live. Being so angry, holding on to every little thing. It makes me realise how forgiveness is at the very heart of the Christian faith, and I'm so thankful for that. We almost take it for granted. Yet it seems like it is a totally alien, even unwelcome, concept to so many. I don't always find forgiveness easy. But unforgiveness is like drinking poison yourself and hoping it kills somebody else. Unforgiveness really is that self-destructive. When I'm hurting sometimes I want to hold on and let everyone know. But by the same token I am so grateful that in Jesus I am forgiven. That He knows me completely, inside and out, and still he loves me. He forgives me. I don't deserve it, but still He offers love, forgiveness and acceptance completely. When I get that straight inside me, not forgiving others doesn't really remain as an option.

# A Place of
# Belonging

*Tuesday 8th September 2009*

Rumours abound that Exeter is going to get our very own flat-pack furniture superstore and honestly it can't be too soon for me. However, as it remains at just that, a rumour, tomorrow I will be driving up the M5 to our currently nearest store. Although the M5 has not been kind to us since we moved to Devon, I'm actually quite looking forward to it as it will give me a day to get to know our new intern, Hannah. She has come to work with us for the year and it will be good to spend some time chatting. More excitingly than that, though, is the reason that we need furniture at all. Because we now have a space for our church in town. It is the back office of one of the city-centre churches, no longer required by the former occupiers. It is only tiny, a mere 5m x 6m, but it also has a toilet and a kitchen of sorts and it is where Unlimited is going to start. We have committed to renting the office for a year. As a family we have donated two futons (not entirely sure why we had two spare futons) but currently there is nothing else. It is up to Hannah and me to provide everything – mugs, plates, cutlery, cushions, pictures, shelves; anything we want to add to make the room seem more comfortable, inviting, accessible – and we have to find it tomorrow. The list seems long and will stretch our limited finances. But there is such joy to finally be doing something so concrete.

## Wednesday 16th September 2009 – am

An inescapable part of reaching young people who don't do church is that if they are not going to come to us, then we are going to have to go to them. Find them where they are and talk to them. I am fully committed to this concept, but today is the first time that I am going to get involved with this side of our mission. The team has been doing this since January. But today, with Toby finally settled in school, I will drive into town, and join in. I am in equal measure excited and terrified. We now have a base in the back office (beautifully decorated with moody black-and-white pictures, cushions and a tufty, green rug) to invite young people back to. In reality it is just an office space, a back room, but we optimistically refer to it as a café. But there is no way a young person will stumble across our wonderful space. As delightful as the furnishings have made it (but honestly, there is only so much a cushion can achieve), the room itself is situated at the dead end of a dank, cobbled alleyway between two imposing buildings. Although this room is such a gift to us, we know that there will be no accidental footfall to this place. It will be God or us or both that draws people in. So for now we will have to go out in pairs and threes to talk to young people.

And therein lies the problem. We will have to go and talk to people. I am shy at the best of times. When you put me in a room of my peers I will be the last to speak, fearful of making a fool of, or calling attention to, myself. This is how I am in a situation when I ought to be confident in who I am, and in any contribution I may make. At the very thought of talking to a teenager, all the negative voices in my head start shouting at why I'm ridiculous to even think about being so bold. 'You are too old. Too frumpy. Too fat. Too boring. Too out of touch. You will speak a different language. You will look a fool.' More insidious was, 'You will make the church and God look even worse. You are a stereotypical Christian and will reinforce all the bad things they already think.'

## Wednesday 16th September 2009 – pm

I survived! I wasn't eaten alive! I might even go so far as to say I enjoyed it. Before we went out to talk to people we prayed together as a group, and it was in that prayer time that I realised we all felt the same. Sure, the little voices, the particular ways in which we were being brought down were specific to each of us. But each of us felt inadequate to the task ahead, and each of us needed to put ourselves aside, and focus instead on God. Because it was with Him and through Him that any of this was going to happen. If He had called me, then for whatever reason I was the right person for the job that day, and I needed to trust more in Him and argue less about why He was wrong. For His ways are not my ways[15] ... I don't get it. But it's OK that I don't get it, as long as I remember to trust and obey.

So we went out in pairs. One person would start the conversation and begin to build a relationship, and the other would be praying (in their head, not out loud) for the conversation until it got to the point where it was right to join in, or move on. At first it was terrifying. I expected to be refused and ridiculed at every encounter, but quickly found that the conversations were fun and enlivening and I could speak without making an utter fool of myself. As it was a lovely sunny afternoon, the Green around the cathedral was packed with young people taking a break from college and uni. There were so many people to talk to. And to my total surprise they seemed very happy to talk to us. That afternoon not one young person was rude, mocked us or refused to talk to us. It was absolutely the opposite of the opposition and hostility that I was expecting. I know that if a strange person came and interrupted my friends and me mid-conversation I would be deeply suspicious and unwelcoming. But thankfully they were not like me.

We were totally honest in our conversation. We started talking to them about their preconceived ideas of church, and of God, and if they were interested in coming to visit a church or discover a God that probably didn't fit their stereotype. In all the groups I spoke to this afternoon, the young people were happy to talk us and in return we respected their views. My hope is in time that we will be able to give them a safe place to explore faith and God,

---

[15] See Isaiah 55:8.

without any pressure. But I know that will stem from relationship, not just one conversation. We also want to offer to pray for them. To show them something about God's nature, how He knows and loves each of us as individuals.

And so it was this afternoon I had one of my strangest experiences of praying. While James and I sat and listened to God, Josh and Stacey played a U2 song. We had met them sitting under a tree on the Green, Josh playing a guitar and Stacey singing along. The fact that it was a U2 song had drawn in James. He is totally unmusical in every way, apart from a lifelong abiding passion for the music of U2. It gave him an easy starter to his conversation and we carried on chatting to them for nearly an hour. We left them eventually with cards where we had written down stuff that we thought God wanted them to hear that day. We had tentatively shared it with them, telling them that we don't always get it right, and they had seemed mainly positive and when we left seemed genuinely interested in meeting us again next week. Especially when we offered hot chocolate mountains and cakes.

## Wednesday 23rd September 2009

They came! Josh and Stacey actually came to café. We had two real, live young people in our back room drinking chocolate mountains and eating angel cake. They hadn't managed to locate us. As we feared, we are sufficiently tucked away that it is almost impossible to find us, even when you are trying. But we bumped into them as they were looking for us. I don't think it was luck. Or coincidence. I think God helped us all be in the right place at the right time. And the rest, as they say, is history. The stayed for the whole afternoon. They ate, they drank, they sang, they chatted. They are coming back next week.

## Saturday 16th January 2010

The kitchen is full of glorious smells. No one is allowed to nibble at the cooling cakes. I have been baking again. The boys all think it is terribly unfair but the cakes are not for them. They are for the family service in Garden Church tomorrow.

This is a new service that our family started in addition to the other services in church. We so wanted to encourage families to come, to provide place for chatter, for sharing life. The church is in need of new life, and something new was needed. I think the congregation were pleased not to have lost anything they held dear and so have been generous and supportive of this new service, despite it not being how they personally would choose to worship. We have tried to gently change things from the formal, familiar liturgy to a service that is open and accessible to families with young children. It is a real family affair. James leads and talks. He always produces a talk that connects with everyone from young to old. I don't know how he does it. I'm always amazed that he can communicate with the very youngest child without patronising the eldest. I play keys and sing the songs. The boys willingly (or sometimes unwillingly) perform the actions when required. Slowly but surely, as word spreads, numbers are increasing.

There is only one point of conflict between us and some of the congregation. Surprisingly it is not the new modern worship that offends the most, the noise, the informal liturgy or the fact that James is not wearing robes. Where the two sides simply cannot agree is on the matter of refreshments. Despite the fact that coffee and drinks are not an easy task, and will be made no easier with increasing numbers, this is not the issue. As there is no water in the church, huge bottles of it have to be brought – filled at home, transported and then carried up the church path. With more families starting to come, this task gets ever harder. But they don't mind the sheer effort of providing drinks. Or even escorting the younger people on the short walk over to the vicarage to make use of the facilities if they really can't wait until they get home (no water means definitely no toilet). No. Their real objection is to the cake. To a few, cake has the potential both to make mess and to ruin people's appetites for their Sunday lunch. They are right in part. In previous months there has been a lot of cake scattered on the floor. It did take a long time to clear up. But honestly I would prefer a messy church as the aftermath of a service that had been full of people, than an empty (but clean) museum. But I can't agree with them on the subject of appetites lost. In my experience, children are always hungry. It appears we come from different generations and our entirely different approaches to food and snacking seems insurmountable. Sadly, last month we reached a stand-off. The ladies on the rota refused to serve the cake that I had made. Full boxes were returned to me after the service with the claim that it was not wanted.

However, James and I are nothing if not determined. I want to provide cake to make people feel welcome and loved, and to let them know that someone cares that they have turned up on a Sunday morning. I want them to know that they are worth more to me than just opening a packet of chocolate biscuits to serve with the instant coffee. I want to make people feel welcomed, looked after, valued. Maybe cake doesn't do all of that, but it is certainly a start. Receiving something for nothing is countercultural. They would happily pay for cake in a coffee shop, and yet we are choosing to give it away for free. So I've made cake again this month. James has tried through many conversations to encourage the church that cake is a good thing. I'm really hoping that this time it will be served.

## Wednesday 20th January 2010

Today a group of young people did not want to talk to us. We went and asked if we could talk to them, and quite rudely they told us 'no'. It was what I had initially expected would be the standard response. However, as all the conversations that I've been part of have been so warm and welcoming, it was today's reaction that felt strange. So cold. So out of the blue. I find it odd that my expectations have shifted so far ... that I now expect to be welcomed into strangers' conversations, and it is the rejection that feels wrong.

## Wednesday 24th February 2010

We have changed the way we talk to young people on the Cathedral Green. No, that's not quite true. We haven't changed what we say. But we have changed whom we say it to. A year ago we happily went up to any youth, but now we are starting to ask God to highlight who we should talk to before we go out. The idea being that we want to go to people where God is already at work. We want to join in with Him on His mission. It's not easy and we often get it wrong. However, when you find yourself having a conversation with someone whom God highlighted to you before you met, it is so encouraging. Today was my first experience of this type of prayer. As a team we prayed before our Wednesday café and I had a picture of a young couple on the cathedral steps, one with long hair and a beard and the sense someone was French. As I remained in church to serve hot chocolate and cake, a team went straight out to the steps and got into conversation and ended up praying for a couple. The guy had long hair, a beard and was called Beau – his family are French. I still can't quite believe that God called us to that couple. That it was that easy. We don't know why that happened today. They didn't come back to café, we may never know the result of that conversation or that prayer. But we do know that today God wanted us to talk to that couple, and we were faithful.

## Sunday 28th March 2010

Egg? Chicken? The fact is we only have two people, Josh and Stacey, and their occasional friends coming to our Wednesday café, and the back room is amply big enough for us all. But I can't stop thinking of the verse in Isaiah where the Lord says, 'Enlarge the place of your tent, stretch your tent curtains wide, do not hold back; lengthen your cords, strengthen your stakes.'[16] Should we wait for more people until we find a bigger place? Do we find a bigger

---

[16] Isaiah 54:2.

place and hope more people will come? Chicken? Egg? I have no idea.

## Wednesday 14th April 2010

Tonight was the final rehearsal before the orchestral concert tomorrow. I have loved rediscovering long-buried skills. The joy of classical music and the shared endeavour with others have been a delight. But tonight was different as 'the professional' was coming. I am only harp 2, a fact for which I am very grateful. I am not the best, and there is no expectation that I should be the best, or indeed better than I am. They are paying another harpist to play the significantly more difficult harp 1 part. I was in such a dither before she came. I had not played for more years than I could count in front of anyone who understood anything about the harp. She could take one look at me and my technique and demolish me with a sentence. It was like going back to school and sitting an exam for which you know you are woefully underprepared, not really having any clue of the scope of the exam. I did not even know the etiquette. Does the principal harpist sit on the left or the right? Desperate not to offend this super-scary, diva-like monster that I had imagined her to be, I set myself up in the middle of nowhere, thinking this may hide my ignorance of orchestral protocol.

When she arrived, Emma was nothing like I expected. She was fun, she was encouraging. She was a brilliant harpist, but in a way that encouraged me to aspire to be better rather than crushed and demoralised. At one point I blurted out that I don't listen to classical music much, and she laughingly agreed. We had a great time. She even offered for us to get together to play duets. Obviously I will never accept. But still it was kind of her to offer.

## Wednesday 21st April 2010

I have to confess that I have been finding café harder and harder. I have a real battle to make myself turn up on a Wednesday. I am determined not to hide behind a label of 'shy', but I find talking to anybody I don't know an effort. It is definitely out of my comfort zone. I find it even harder talking to the young people in the café. We have very few points of contact in common. I don't know their friends, their college, their music, their apps. I don't even understand their language (dating and going out are apparently totally different concepts – who knew?). But up until today, staying in the café has been an infinitely preferable option to going out on to the Cathedral Green.

My reluctance to go out on to the Green doesn't entirely make sense, even to me, because when I have gone out I've had some amazing conversations and encounters. In the main the young people are friendly and willing to talk to us. Yet something in me would much prefer to avoid going out on the Green. I've shared my struggles with James. In fact it would have been impossible to hide from him how I'm really feeling. He has been patient. Endlessly encouraging me to persevere. But it hasn't seemed to get any easier.

In time spent with God I have begun to realise that I'm not always unwilling to go out on the Green. I enjoy going out when I am paired with someone who I know will initiate the conversation, but I really struggle when I am expected to lead. I find it so difficult to approach groups and initiate conversations, and often catch myself making excuses as to why we shouldn't bother one group or another. And it seems I am not alone, I am not the only one who has been finding Wednesdays difficult. Some of the team have been talking to me about how they too struggle to start conversations. It's not true for everyone. Some team members love it. They love bouncing up to new people and talking to them.

So James and I have come to the conclusion that the most successful pairs that go out and talk to young people contain two types of people: initiators and supporters. He is definitely an initiator. I am most emphatically a supporter. We make a great team. It is a joy to go out with him. And for many pairs this model happens naturally, but it doesn't always. Often when I am paired with a younger team member they see me as Liz, leader of the church, older, wiser, more capable. They think that if they are paired with me then I will take a lead. And that fear of being forced into initiating was making me try to avoid going out at all. And I probably wasn't alone.

So today as we prayed and organised ourselves into pairs, we asked the team who felt comfortable in which roles, and ensured each team had an initiator and a supporter. It was such a relief. With the defined roles I felt released to seek God out on the Green. I was much happier in the prayer support role, and now having this recognised has taken off so much pressure. I can look at groups and pray about whether we should approach them without my stuff getting in the way (by my stuff, I mean all the reasons I would come up with as to why we shouldn't!). I know that I can join in a conversation where I am not the lead and I love the privilege of praying for the youth at the end of an encounter.

It is such a simple change, and so in line with our heartbeat, that longs to see a church full of people released to be who they are, released with their strengths, rather than all of us trying to fill the gaps, that I'm surprised we haven't done it before. It has changed my attitude totally to Wednesday cafés and the encounters I may have. I am full of hope and excitement. I know that God will use me as I am. I don't have to try to be something I'm not.

## Tuesday 27th April 2010

I am going to Emma's house today. We had a really great time playing together in the orchestra and we are going to have a coffee together. She thinks I could earn money as a harpist. She plays at weddings, and has too many bookings. She would like to be able to pass on her double bookings to someone rather than let a bride down. I don't think I could do it, I'm nowhere near as skilled as she is. But I'll go and hear what she has to say.

# 'Enlarge the Place of Your Tent'[17]

## Wednesday 28th April 2010

On the one hand it feels crazy and on the other hand it feels so right. We have started to rent the main space of Mary Arches Church for our Wednesday café. We rent it just for the afternoon. Although it is just a few small steps down a dark corridor from our usual location, it feels much further. Today we rattled around in the church. Josh, Stacey and the team. We were awkward. The easy camaraderie of the back room was gone. The piano proved a welcome distraction. But there was no getting round the fact that Josh and Stacey did not like it, and no one else came. I hope we are doing the right thing.

---

[17] Isaiah 54:2.

## Wednesday 12th May 2010

Much of what we do at church is uncomfortable to me. I don't know that the thought of going out and talking to people I have never met before will ever become comfortable, but I do know it is the right thing to do. I was talking to a girl last week, and she seemed genuinely grateful of an opportunity to talk about what church was and who God is. She told me that she had never been able to have such a conversation before. There was no one in her family that went to church, and none of her friends went either. I was literally the first Christian that she had been able to talk to. I was shocked that this was the case, but felt privileged and grateful that I was given the opportunity to talk to her.

So this week I decided to step out further and be the one initiating conversation. It was made slightly more terrifying as Ed was accompanying me. Ed had come for the afternoon to check us out as a church. He is nearing the end of his first year studying theology and is looking for a church to settle in for the rest of his time at university. While in my head I know that it is all about God and not about me, I confess that in my heart I desperately didn't want to make a fool of myself in front of him, but I also wanted him to see how exciting our mission is. In the end nothing miraculous happened. We had a few good conversations. We returned to church. As we walked back I was relieved that it was over. I had stepped up and not fallen flat on my face. Ed was encouraging and promised to return after the long summer break. I hope he doesn't forget us in all the months that he will be away.

## Wednesday 2nd June 2010

Holding the café in church still seems strange. We only have a small team, no more than seven of us if we all manage to make it, and there is so much to do. Before we can even start we have to clear away what is already there. Rows and rows of chairs. Then carry through every single thing we want in café. Every cup, cake, plate, beanbag, board game must be collected from the back room. Everything has to be carried along the dark corridor and placed in an inviting manner in the church. There are no pews, just a big, empty space and each week it feels like we are reinventing the wheel as we try to remember what looks good, works well, aids conversation and connection, and what doesn't. The floor has been disappointingly covered in a dull, brown carpet that feels more like Velcro than anything soft and comforting. The walls are covered with ancient monuments with three-dimensional statues, skulls and even a dog. We, the team, have long since stopped seeing these alien oddities and yet each week it needs to be fresh in our mind what first impression are we giving. What the church feels like when they enter is so important. We want it to feel welcoming, friendly and inviting. We want them to be at their ease, and so each week we try to create a space for them that is familiar and recognisable and not too foreign.

At the end of the afternoon everything must be restored to how it was before. The church regains its quiet silence. The rows of chairs are replaced. We hope the parishioners whose church we borrow hardly notice that we have been there. Our beanbags, crockery, foodstuffs are returned to the back room. This room is still the base of our church. Everything we possess is crammed into every nook and cranny. It is used several times a week for smaller meetings, and the space needs to remain attractive and inviting. We do not want it to feel like a cross between a store cupboard and a junkyard. It is a lot of work, but we are being joined just for three months by the endlessly encouraging and energetic David. While they work out what lies ahead, he and his wife, Charis, have joined the team. They bring fresh eyes, fresh vision, fresh enthusiasm. They give the whole team much love and we are so grateful for them.

Strange though it still seems, it seems to be working. Week by week more people are coming to café. Some weeks four. Some weeks six. Never more than ten. But they are coming, and they keep coming back.

## Wednesday 9th June 2010

I sometimes wonder why we pray for young people. Does it make any difference? Why do we bother? I can't answer these imponderables except that I do know that we don't understand the full effects of our mission and our calling. We have now prayed for more than 100 young people, and God has spoken into their lives, shown them personally that they are loved and known to him. At that moment of great vulnerability we have to be so careful. We don't want to pressure them into making a decision that is not thought through or real. Our longing is for them to know God and know that He loves them. It is a journey that we need to work out with them.

Take this afternoon – one of our team came back with a story of praying for two young people. At the end of chat they offered prayer and the two boys accepted. As Hannah prayed, she had a sense that the lad shared a room with his sister. It felt a bit weird since he must have been around seventeen, so, rather than asking directly, she asked whether he shared a room with a sibling. When he said he did, she asked if it was his sister. He was shocked that she could possibly know this and it turned out, as he explained to her, that at his dad's place there was only one room, so he had to share with his sister.

Quite quickly after that prayer the encounter finished and the boys left. We have gently invited them to café, and told them how to seek us out another time, but many will not. We take their names back, record them in a book and faithfully pray for them. But we do not know the effect that the prayers have. Many of the people that we pray for are from all over Devon. They come to Exeter for college, but their lives, friends and communities are miles away from us. We have to trust them to God. He is leading us to them and speaking into their lives for a reason. When I don't understand I am reminded of the verse in Hebrews: 'Now faith is confidence in what we hope for and assurance about what we do not see.'[18]

## Saturday 10th July 2010

Today has been a very odd day. I was uniquely privileged to be invited to the wedding of Eve and Tim. I'd never met them before the day. I was not invited as a guest but as

---

[18] Hebrews 11:1.

their harpist. Emma had a double booking and convinced me that I could stand in for her. I've never been to a wedding where I am not a guest and, as lovely and welcoming as the families are, it felt odd. I was not there to have a good time. I was not there to drink the champagne (which they offered freely and abundantly – perhaps completely unaware that I would be unable to play a note after the first few sips!). I'm not ready to call myself a professional harpist yet. I don't know if I can make a career out of this. I do know, however, that I love playing the harp. To be paid for doing so seems a little unfair. Over the last year and a half I have rediscovered how much I enjoy playing the harp, making music. I love the concentration and discipline that it requires. More than that, though, music to me seems to be part of the human soul. God has hard-wired us to worship Him. Not with music alone, but certainly music is part of that. Somewhere along the years I had lost sight of the richness and depth and beauty of music. It has been a journey in skills remembered, things once second nature being relearned, and it has been a pure delight.

## Tuesday 10th August 2010

I am not a fan of mobile phones. No, that's not true. They are brilliant in their place. The problem for us is that their place is everywhere. There is literally nowhere we can go and not be contactable. James loves it. In his love of people, he never wants to miss out. He wants to be the first to know everything. It gives him a reassurance that people can get hold of him, that he can go to them when they need him. I love that in him, his compassion for others. But I hate the fact that it leaves me today with two small children in a rain-battered caravan, with no car, in north Cornwall. It is not the weather that was unexpected. Anyone who chooses a summer holiday in Cornwall has to be prepared for four seasons every day. But I was not expecting to be here alone. We had only been on holiday for a few days when we heard that a very dear friend, and a churchwarden in one of James' five churches, had died unexpectedly. He and his wife had been so very kind to us when we moved down and knew no one, and I can only imagine the pain that she is feeling at the moment. I'm glad that my husband loves them enough to put his own self aside and go to her at her time of greatest need. I know I would want the same love shown to me if I was ever in that place. But I can't help but wonder if this is a good thing for us as a family. We can't ever switch off. We are always on call. It is the modern world.

## Friday 3rd September 2010

David and Charis have left us, called on to their next adventure. I miss David's smiling encouragement. His energy. His exuberance. I miss Charis' open-hearted love and acceptance of the many young girls that she connected with in church. We knew they would only be with us for a short time. We would have loved for it to be longer.

## Wednesday 8th September 2010

It's no longer practical to ask the team to come to our house on Tuesday evenings. Five people travelling from Exeter out to our village no longer seems fair when the two of us,

James and I, could travel instead. I am sad because I think almost everything about our home is better than church. It is warm, cosy, inviting, comfortable. Almost the antithesis of the back room of Mary Arches, which is where we will now meet, although we have tried so hard for that not to be the case. How I wish we lived nearer so that we didn't have to make this decision. However, we finally have enough support in the village for us to leave the boys at home with babysitters while we two travel into Exeter. Mary, Mary and Heather don't come to Unlimited, are committed to other churches, but want to support us in any way they can. I am deeply grateful. The boys will be loved, and we are free to go out.

We met last night. This year we will meet every Tuesday night as a team. It will be an evening of prayer and worship. A time to learn, to be discipled, to deepen our relationship with God.

## Wednesday 15th September 2010

It is my turn this week to bake the cakes for Wednesday. I don't really have time. I need to catch up on my jobs, and I've been invited out for coffee. I haven't spent enough time with the children. But I just have to put that aside. We so want to show young people that we care enough to put time and effort into providing good stuff for them. Many of them don't even get meals cooked for them at home, so the fact that someone would bother to make a cake for them is special. Better get the recipe out. Twenty-four chocolate chip muffins, here we come!

## Friday 17th September 2010

Had such fun playing harp duets today. Initially I felt so self-conscious, thinking this would be like the worst ever lesson, with every fault minutely picked over. Emma, however, is much more gracious than that. In fact, she is just a genuine enthusiast for all things harp and seems honestly excited to have someone to share her delight with. I'm not her equal. But we have fun and I don't disgrace myself.

## Wednesday 22nd September 2010

I'm delighted that Ed remembered his promise of the early summer. He has returned and looks set to stay. We now have a solid team of eight: James and myself, Steve and Helen, four students, Alison, Jess, Ruth and Ed. At café today it was good to see some young people returning. I was worried that after the break they would forget, or move on to the next thing. But this was not the case. In particular two girls, Jess and Katy, seem more and more committed. Each week they spend time with Steve and Helen, reading the Bible and talking about faith and God. Each week they draw a little closer to us and to God.

# Toastie Sundays

## Sunday 7th November 2010

Unlimited held its first service tonight. We have wanted to start a Sunday service for a long time, yet we were determined to start the church around the young people who came to faith within Unlimited, and so we have had to be patient. At times it felt too hard to wait, especially as we have seen people come and go and slip away to join more 'conventional' churches. But we have tried to be faithful. We had church today because Jess and Katy have become Christians, and we built a service around them.

The service was very short. Well, it was about an hour, which probably felt a long time for Jess and Katy, but felt very short to me. We based it around food, with the knowledge that the early Church met with food. With no kitchen at church, our options were limited, but I was pleased with the idea of toasted sandwiches. With a choice of cheese, ham or cheese and ham we all received a plateful and sat and ate together. Jess commented that 'this must be what family feels like' and I just knew that we had got it right. That is exactly what God has called us to be for Jess and Katy. Family. After food, there was a video, a short thought from James, an opportunity to pray or be prayed for, and one worship song played by Ed on a guitar. The basics of church stripped down to a minimum. I hope in time it will be more, that it will develop. But for now it is right for us as a church.

We will meet again as church in one month for 'Toastie Sunday'. It seemed a long way away as we closed the door on our first-ever service.

## Monday 13th December 2010

I feel as if we are always driving. I worked out that last week James and I each drove to Exeter every day for Unlimited. Sometimes we go to meet young people for coffee. Or we meet up with team members for mentoring or prayer. We have prayer meetings, leadership meetings, café. Every day now there is something connected with church that we need to attend. A sixteen-mile round trip, seven days a week, two cars. We can't sustain this. We can't build a church if we don't live there. We can't casually invite people round for a cup of tea, to pop in. We can't just hang out and do life together. Everything needs to be preplanned. We always have to go to them. It doesn't feel natural. It is completely exhausting. Something has to change.

## Friday 14th January 2011

Same story: James is working too hard. There is simply too much for him to do. Between the five parishes and the people based there, and the city-centre youth, it feels like we never see him. He is being pulled in every direction and we just have to stand and watch. He is pretty good at being home for dinner and the start of bedtime, but it is the rare evening when he is not straight out again. I honestly don't know how much longer he can sustain this. It is time to talk to the bishop again.

On Tuesday nights the team have spent the last few meetings praying about our vision, our values, our calling. I think James and I have known what they are for a long time, but we have been verbose and informal in our explanations. As a group we have taken the rambling explanations and honed them to something sleek and succinct. Somehow they have made Unlimited more real, more focused, more exciting. Just words. But such power behind them.

Our mission is simple. 'Young people encountering the God they've never met and living the difference.' The picture that we have is of a race, as the writer to the Hebrews described in his letter.[19] Each of us has our own race set before us. We can't run someone else's race, simply our own. We need to know our own race, we need to pursue the life that God has given us. And to run freely and effectively we need to get rid of all the stuff that holds us back and weighs us down. We need to deal with stuff that is wrong in our lives. And then we need to fix our eyes on Jesus – who began it all and will complete it all. Simple. Exciting.

Our values unpack why we are called Unlimited. It's a good name. But it has always been more than just an empty

---

[19] Hebrews 12:1-2.

word. We truly want to be unlimited. Unlimited by church culture and tradition – where it is unhelpful, unnecessary or inappropriate. Unlimited in our openness to and love of people – treating them as unique and as God has made them to be. Unlimited in our faith and expectation of God – living by faith, not inhibited by past experience or fears.

So James will go to the bishop to ask him to review his dual role. This time, though, he goes with six churches in his portfolio. Five from the parish ministry, and Unlimited.

## Wednesday 9th February 2011

I'm enjoying not having to dash away from café this year. Since we started, I have had to keep one eye on the clock during every encounter, every conversation, every prayer time. Always having to be so aware that I must be back in Rockbeare to pick up my children from school. But not so any more. I am free to stay as long as I want. It is a luxury. I have been given the gift of time. I am so grateful. The boys now actively look forward to Wednesdays, rather than worry I will be late, again. They are met from school by Heather, our wonderful churchwarden in Rockbeare, who has become an unexpected but very dear friend. She is like a granny to the boys and is a blessing to us all. The boys cherish their time with her. She gives them a freedom to explore and create. Maybe more importantly, to them at least, there is also amazing food. She and her husband make and sell organic bread at farmers' markets across Devon. They have freezers full, and Josh seems determined to try every flavour. They also have great fun together making concoctions. The perfect concoction involves choosing literally anything edible you want from

Heather's garden and putting it in a smoothie maker. She doesn't refuse them anything. She doesn't try to bend them around to her way of thinking. She lets them design their own triumphs, and occasionally, disasters. They love her confidence in their abilities. In the summer they have free range of her garden, her fruit, her herbs. She is endlessly generous, and even if I don't fancy a vanilla, raspberry, currant, mint and basil ice cream concoction, then I am in the minority. They love it, and when I arrive weary and talked-out from café I am greeted with a glass for my considered opinion. This is followed by a cup of tea and some quiet restoration in front of her Aga before I take the children home to continue the evening routine.

Wednesday café numbers fluctuate between five and fifteen people. Young people who don't have any experience of church are being brought along by their friends who equally have no experience of church. They have just met us and they like us. We have prayed for them all at least once. We don't force them to have prayer, but we aim never to let a young person leave after a second visit without us at least offering. On the one hand the numbers aren't huge, but on the other it does mean that we can really get to know them. Listen to their stories. Many stories are heartbreaking to me. One lad and his mum were made homeless in the middle of last year. They had to wait until just before Christmas for housing, and even then they had to wait another six weeks for a cooker. All the while he tried to continue at college. Unsurprisingly his grades suffered. Another girl, also at college, faced the prospect of going into care because her mum allegedly has a degenerative disease. She, however, believes that she is making it up to cheat the benefits system and has now moved in with grandparents. We have had two girls concerned that they might be pregnant. The week before Christmas, one girl told us that her dad had left the day before. One lad was left behind when his dad and stepmother moved away and his stepmother wouldn't take him with them. Two of the girls who come to us are already in care. One girl is currently seeking a place at the YMCA because she cannot cope with her dad's anger.

Sometimes I despair of meeting anyone 'normal'. Because these are the stories we hear all the time. They are not unusual. These young people face more on a day-to-day basis than I can even imagine. Their problems can appear overwhelming, and our resources to help them seem pitiful. But today as one guy left he said to us, 'This is the only time in the week that I feel safe.' I am delighted that we provide a small haven, an oasis, in his week where he can feel safe. But it does not feel enough. There must be more that we can do.

## Thursday 10th February 2011

I did not expect to be in hospital today. I suppose many people walking through the hospital doors had no idea that their day would turn out like this. I had an unfortunate accident involving my thumb and a food processor. Just a cut, they said. Deep but clean. There was no special treatment for me as a harpist. They hope it will heal well. That sensation will return. I'm not convinced. I wasn't a good patient. It turns out I am extremely squeamish, especially when it is my flesh flapping open. Good job I discarded the idea of becoming a doctor early on in life! I can't dwell on that now because I have to focus on what lies ahead. The accident could not have happened at a worse time. I was busy preparing food in advance of the weekend away. I carried on one-handed.

## Sunday 13th February 2011

Tonight I am happy and exhausted in equal measure. I feel full from such an outpouring of God's goodness. We have just returned from a weekend away with the Unlimited team. Ten of us, if you include Josh and Toby. I was worried about this weekend. James and I organised it all, and were responsible for everything. The boys are part of this new church, and it felt right for them to be with us, not sent away for the weekend. But that meant I was cook, Mum, children's worker, Unlimited leader. Every moment was filled. I was in the kitchen, I was praying, I was leading worship, I was chatting. It was all good. But now I am left craving solitude and peace.

# Going All In

*Monday 14th February 2011*

After James met with Bishop Michael a few weeks ago, there were subsequent meetings in the diocese. The result of which is that the Bishop of Exeter and his two suffragans have requested that James should submit a written proposal for Unlimited Church to become a Bishop's Mission Order (BMO). This would give us some formality and accountability while leaving us with a freedom to pursue our vision. In preparing this document for the bishops, we realised that we have prayed for more than 500 young people over the last three years. It sounds an amazing number. Although we aren't always seeing the result of this prayer, it must be having an impact, albeit unseen.

I am excited to think that we might become a BMO. It would clarify who and what we are. Currently, we stand somewhere between being a parachurch outreach and a church. Those on the team are divided between being part of it and also of an established church. We are still regarded suspiciously by other churches. They don't really know what we are and still assume Soul Exeter is the youth church we are seeking to establish. If we became a BMO it would mean that any young person who comes to faith with us can then be nurtured in church with us, in a place that is familiar and recognisable to them. Because you cannot survive as a Christian without fellowship, without meeting other believers. We are instructed in the Bible not to give up meeting with one another.[20] If we cannot be their church, we would have to encourage them elsewhere. It would seem strange to have spent all this time with young people, getting them to revise their opinions of God and church only to turn around and tell them that when they become a Christian they now need to go to somewhere else, to a different church, which inevitably would be more traditional than us.

It has taken a while to get all the paperwork together. But I'm proud of what we have written. I'm excited by all that is to come.

## Tuesday 1st March 2011

Everything is changing. But nothing is certain. It feels as if my head is full of endless possibilities, what ifs. It is as though the uncertainty is filling up all the spare space, all the nooks and crannies in my head, and it is exhausting. I am excited about the next phase of life. But at the moment the prospect of what is to come is stealing the joy of the present. I need to learn to treasure the here and now. I need to learn from Josh and Toby. They know what is

---

[20] Hebrews 10:25.

happening, that we are hoping for Unlimited to become a church, to be Daddy's only job. But for them it is a knowledge that doesn't have an impact on the joy of today. The knowledge is there, but there is no rushing ahead, planning, guessing, dreaming. They live in the present, in what is before them. And I am determined to join them.

## Wednesday 16th March 2011

I love the way that music sticks in our heads. It doesn't matter how great a talk is, I'm unlikely to remember it by Thursday (or honestly perhaps even Monday!). But the songs we've sung will be in my head and heart all week. I'll be humming them in the shower, when I'm driving, when I'm cooking. The words I've sung stay with me in a way that the words I've heard just don't. My earworm at the moment has a bridge that reminds me that when God is on our side, nothing can come against us, nothing can stop us. I take great comfort in those lines. When we sing them as a church there is such power in declaring them together. In the quiet moments during the week they bring me great comfort. I often feel overwhelmed by the task set before us. I feel too small, and there are so many things standing against this church. If I let myself I can panic about us not having enough people, enough time, enough money … the list goes on in a spiral of fear and worry if I let it. But I know that when I start fearing what lies ahead it is because I have taken my eyes off God and started looking only at the obstacles. I have begun relying on my own strength. This song that is stuck in my ear reminds me daily to fix my eyes back on God. Because if we are walking with God then we have nothing to fear. He does not promise that it will be easy. But He does promises always to be with us.

## Friday 15th April 2011

The formal proposal for us to become a BMO has been completed, and so the process begins. Although I know this is a good thing, it feels rather more as though a hurricane has passed through our lives. Everything that we know has been uprooted. When the hurricane has passed I know there will be peace again. But I also know for certain that nothing will look the same. I don't know what the future looks like, but equally I know that we can't return to the past. It is now a foreign land to us, and we have to look forward to what is ahead.

## Tuesday 10th May 2011

My heart is full to overflowing. I am overwhelmed by God's love and generosity. I have a note stuck to the mirror in my bedroom reminding me of a verse from Psalm 37 which says, 'Take delight in the Lord, and he will give you the desires of your heart.'[21] I had always read it as though I had to ask first. As though good behaviour, of doing what God requires of me, would then mean that he blesses me. But today for the first time I think that I have got that verse, and God, completely wrong. Him choosing to bless me is not dependent in any way on me or my actions. It is His choice simply because He loves me. I am completely undeserving, and always will be, no matter what I do.

---

[21] Psalm 37:4.

Today this verse starts to make sense to me because I am amazed at everything that has happened within the last month. While I have struggled to find peace among so many unknowns, God has carried on blessing me. More quickly than we could ever have imagined He has given us a church, a job, a mission. We hopefully have money and a building. Instead of renting Mary Arches Church for each use, the parish have agreed to an annual rent. The dwindling parish congregation have kindly agreed to relocate to a warmer, brighter, more central church nearby for their monthly service. It will be solely our building to do with exactly as we will. No more constantly moving stuff back and forth from the back room. God has provided a school for the boys. He has even opened up a harp teaching job for me. It feels too much, too generous. God has granted me some desires of my heart that I had not even admitted to myself. God's love and generosity are too lofty to get my head around. I will simply delight in Him without understanding Him.

# Highs and Lows

## Sunday 22nd May 2011

Today was such a day of celebration. Jess and Katy got baptised. They publicly told their friends and family the decision that they had made last year, that they believed in God and were going to follow Him with all their hearts. For us as a church it was the first time that we had met their families, and it was so lovely. I think at first they were quite wary of us. It is a big thing when your child comes to tell you they have made a massive life decision, such as deciding to believe in God, especially when it is not a belief that you necessarily share or agree with. I am sure that they wondered who we were, and what we were up to. But I think they went home much happier. Every occasion that we have ever had at church is celebrated with food, and this time we chose party food. Everyone brought something. Mini sausages, crisps, sandwiches. And, of course, cake! Much fuss was made of Jess and Katy and I think their friends and family saw how much we love and care for them and want the very best for them. It was a very special day.

## Sunday 5th June 2011

Toby and I have been the support vehicle today. Even though there were seven of them, and should have been easy to track, it was surprisingly difficult to be in the right place at the right time with water, sustenance and encouragement. Ed, Jess, Ruth, James (Ruth's boyfriend) and Steve had set out yesterday from Ilfracombe on a sponsored cycle ride from the north to south coast of Devon to raise funds to take young people to Soul Survivor. I think my James and Josh were secretly relieved that we could not join them until day two, which was definitely a flatter and easier day. We met them to camp last night at the strangely named Nomansland in mid-Devon. We found a weary bunch. Bikes had not performed well; there was a huge range of cycling ability and speed within the group. The hills had been vicious and stomach bugs had not improved matters.

Things were much better today. James cycled for the whole day. Josh joined them for the first ten miles. He has six gears, and probably only used two of them. He cycled at a slow but steady speed. They were so encouraging; he felt so proud of himself. He did not want to stop but I knew that if the group were ever to reach Exmouth I would have to intervene. In a very unpopular move I took Josh and Toby home for lunch with a promise to meet the group in Exmouth for ice-cream celebrations. When we were reunited mid-afternoon there was great jubilation. Everyone had survived. Everyone had made it across

Devon, against all the odds. More excitingly, their joint venture had raised £1,000. Now we could offer to take young people away to the Soul Survivor festival, and money would not have to be a barrier. We could offer them a week of holiday. A week for them to escape their difficult home situations, their day-to-day lives, and be immersed in God. Learning about Him and living with people 24/7 who love Him and want to share that love.

## Tuesday 14th June 2011

Today we have to say goodbye to our student, Jess, and I feel a little as though my heart is breaking. In the three years that we have known her she has become a part of our family. She has taught the boys to swim. She has read with them, played with them, loved them. She lived with us for a few weeks when she needed a break from the intensity of university. We have laughed, cried and prayed together. With her I have started to learn how to mother the people that God is bringing to church. She is leaving at the end of her degree to join another church, to be their intern. I wish she could stay with us, that we had the money to fund a position for her. But it is not right. She is called on her own walk with God and she has prayerfully listened to Him for what she should do next. I know that it is right that she should leave. But it doesn't make it any easier, being the ones left behind. It will feel strange continuing the Unlimited journey without her. And yet, we know that she must go. And we must be happy for her. And make it easy for her, release her with joy for all that she has been, and leave no trace of guilt that she is leaving when our need is so great. I'm trying to do all that. Not all the family are succeeding. Toby cannot accept that she is leaving. He refuses to even try to be happy for her. He cannot face her. He calls her 'the abandoner'. I can't console him at all.

## Friday 22nd July 2011

We haven't found it easy living in the village at all times, but it was with real sadness that we walked home from school for the last time today. Although we are not moving until Christmas, the boys will start the next school year, come September, in their new school. For one last time we paused on the little humpback bridge over the river and watched the water chuckling merrily below. Josh has left behind nearly five years of friendship, fun, nurture and he is feeling it. It was his decision to change schools at this stage. But the fact that the decision was his does not make it any easier. He does not like change. The small, three-classroomed school has suited him perfectly. He has flourished, and although it is time for him to stretch his wings, today holds nothing of the excitement of new beginnings, just the sadness of good things drawing to a close. Toby has not been at the school for as many years, and his time has not been as happy or positive, and yet he too is subdued and saddened by all that we have left behind. Next term their friends will be returning, streaming into the sunny classroom at the beginning of September with tales of happy holidays, and they will be starting in a strange place with a new uniform. The outsiders. The new boys.

We have a quiet evening. There are a few tears at bedtime. Thankful for all that we have had in this village. Sad for all that we are leaving behind.

## Thursday 28th July 2011

Ruth has just got engaged! Her fiancé, James, works in an outdoor activity centre on Dartmoor. They seem perfectly matched. Both love sport, exercise and the outdoors. But they are also great fun, encouraging and wholehearted in all that they do. They bring wisdom, laughter and compassion in equal measure. James has been coming with Ruth to our Tuesday night meetings, but he is currently fully committed to another church in Exeter. Presumably in time that will have to change. One of them will have to move churches. They will need to start worshipping together. We don't want to prejudice their decision. They must go where is right for them. I really hope it is with us.

## Monday 1st August 2011

I can't believe the timing. In the middle of the consultation process, just as everything looks set to proceed, we have had a formal complaint made against us. A parent has written to the bishop complaining about Unlimited Church. The complaint is that we are preying on unsuspecting youth in the city. They are worried that our prayers are unhelpful and manipulative at best, at worst that we are offering the equivalent of horoscopes. They are concerned for vulnerable youth that we may come into contact with.

I am devastated. I don't know how we should defend ourselves. As a parent I can to some extent understand her concern. I am fiercely protective of my children and passionately want the best for them. I understand that. But how best to respond? To allay fears? We just don't know what to say.

## Sunday 7th August 2011

After a week of prayer and advice, James has replied. Without being defensive he tried to explain who we are and what we do. I have since found out that because they lacked any way to contact us (totally our fault), they sent the letter to a former vicar of Mary Arches who denied all knowledge of our existence and agreed with all the parents' concerns and advised them to take it further! So I'm not surprised they were worried by what they had heard.

One of their concerns was how we made contact with young people in the first place, so James explained the café set-up and that we also go on to the Cathedral Green to talk to young people, but that we always check that they are happy to chat. James then tried to explain that we do it because we believe that at the heart of Christian faith is relationship with God and that God knows and loves all of us. He said that young people these days know very little about Christianity and are not often interested in an intellectual discussion about it, but they might want to know why it might be relevant to them. So we offer to pray for them, not as a gimmick or act of clairvoyance, but in the belief that God speaks (although we said that we are always tentative that we are actually hearing Him). James then explained that the team will tell the young person that what they share may be wrong or may just be intuition, but that something of it may also be from God. They check that the young people are comfortable with being prayed for before they do so. They never share anything negative, critical or directive for someone's future. Afterwards, they check that the young people are happy with what's been shared and reiterate that they should only accept what they are comfortable with. They don't probe or try to get any kind of response from them, recognising that such prayer can leave people a bit exposed and vulnerable.

There was much else in the letter. He apologised for any distress and offered to meet if that would be helpful. His words were carefully chosen, wise and kind. I don't know how they will be received. But we have been as honest as we can. I hope that is enough.

## Tuesday 30th August 2011

Tomorrow school starts again. It seems wrong for term to start in August! We have barely recovered from our camping trip. I've only just waded through the washing mountain and caught up on many hours of lost sleep. I'm always sad at the end of the summer holidays. I so enjoy having the boys at home. For long, sunny days with nothing that needs to be done or achieved. Just time spent together, doing nothing special.

Of course, we have been away. We took our first group of young people to Soul Survivor, including Jess and Katy. Everything was a new experience to them and, as we arrived at a muddy site, having to pitch unfamiliar tents in the persistent drizzle, I have to admit to wondering if we had made a huge mistake. Everything was a culture shock to them. Nothing felt safe. I was worrying needlessly. They quickly discovered the marketplace, the cafés, the places to hang out. They adapted to the daily rhythm of meals and meetings and ridiculously long queues for the shower. We all had a brilliant time. Much fun. Not much sleep. But in the words of Jess, we all 'drew closer to God'.

So today we have checked the new uniform. Thankfully they haven't grown out of it. We check bags and pencil cases. Everything is ready. New school tomorrow.

# Sunday Gatherings

## Sunday 4th September 2011

We became a bit more traditional today. A bit more recognisable as a church. We started a weekly service on a Sunday. Until we move house it means that we have to drive in from the village to the centre of Exeter. There will not be much time for family on a Sunday. James will spend his mornings in the parish, join us for a quick lunch, and then we will all head into the city. To start with it will just be the four of us regularly moving the chairs, finding beanbags, putting out mugs and cake, sorting out the sound. Others will join us when they can, but we know the responsibility starts and ends with us. James will lead and speak. He will tailor the talks to who is actually there. Ed and I will share the worship. We want to stick to our values, to be unlimited by culture or tradition. I think this means that this church probably won't look like any other church that I have ever been to. I kind of think that I shouldn't feel 100 per cent comfortable in Unlimited, or certainly not to start with. We want the service to feel relevant, accessible and engaging. We want to shape the service around the young people who come, not ourselves. Everything we do wants to point to God, and we are free to do that in any way that we can. It is an incredibly generous freedom that we have been granted by the Church of England. I hope we are up to it.

Now that we have a Sunday service, something that looks a bit more like church rather than missional outreach, it has forced James and Ruth into making a decision about church rather sooner than they expected. It doesn't make sense to come to us on a Tuesday night and not to come to us on a Sunday. The gatherings are not either/or. You have to be fully in or fully out. Wherever you choose to worship you need to commit wholeheartedly, and they know it. With a tinge of sadness on James' part and great joy on ours, they have decided to commit to Unlimited. Now we are eight.

## Tuesday 20th September 2011

I know that becoming a BMO is exciting. But I have to confess that sometimes I don't find the actual process much fun. Often it seems like endless meetings and discussion, without much progress. Tuesday nights have become consumed with this process. But tonight we made a big step forward. We have been debating for a time whether or not we should set up Unlimited as a company limited by guarantee or as a charitable trust. We have to choose one option or the other as we need to make ourselves into a legal entity. Hence lengthy discussion and research into which fits us better. Finally the choice became clear. The legal minimum age of a company director is sixteen, whereas to be a trustee for a charity you have to be eighteen. If we are serious about youth church, about being a church whose focus is sixteen- to eighteen-year-olds, then it seems obvious that we need to at least be able to have them involved in leadership. There may only be a few exceptional young people whom it would be right to ask to join the leadership, in the capacity of directors, but it seems obvious to all of us that we must allow this as an option. So the decision is made. We are to be a company.

As a company we will have a leadership made up of directors and a church congregation formally known as company members. Attendees of Unlimited will have the choice to sign up as members. But this means we have also had to decide exactly what it means to be a member of Unlimited Church. I think we all sort of knew what we thought it meant but, as numbers increased and the vision began to extend, there was a real need to formalise those thoughts. I don't enjoy the process. But I love the result. The words we scripted together are succinct. They leave no room for error. In my world they feel black and white and I like that. I'm proud of what our meetings have produced. To become a member of our church means that you want to belong, but you also are publicly declaring that you support our vision and values, that you have to be baptised and are committed to growing as a disciple of Christ, that you will attend regularly, that you will actively serve the mission of the church, and that you will give to it.

We will start with a membership in single figures. But it will grow.

## Tuesday 1st November 2011

The house that we will move to became empty today. The tenants moved out and the diocesan builders moved in. Before today we had only seen the house once. It was on a hot, sunny day and the visit was desperately uncomfortable. We were accompanied through every room by the archdeacon, the estate agent and the tenant. There was no chance to discuss what might go where, what colours we fancied. We had to take it all in and try to remember everything to discuss later, privately. Inevitably things had changed shape and size in our minds. On my visit today I was delighted to find that there was room for table and chairs in the kitchen. James had promised me that there would be, but I had remained unconvinced until I had seen it for myself. However, that was pretty much the only part of the visit that was delightful. With the exit of the tenants, the extent of the work needing to be undertaken was staggering. The diocese are responsible for substantial building works, partitioning off the third floor which will remain accessible but hopefully better insulated, creating a study, giving us a new bathroom. But everything else fell to us. Floors, ceiling, windows and walls. All our responsibility. The house is huge. Built in 1803, it is a vast Georgian rectory. It has high ceilings and generous rooms. It will be amazing. It will be a beautiful house, a great place to live. But today as I walked through the house all I could see was that every wall needed stripping, repapering and painting. Every window frame needed glossing. The floors need to be sanded and varnished as we simply can't afford the vast acreage of carpet.

We barely have two months before we plan to move. We are going to very busy.

## Saturday 12th November 2011

I often wonder what happens to the young people that we pray for. As much as we encourage them to come along to café, to keep talking to us, the truth is that the majority never do. We keep on praying for them. We know it is about sowing seeds rather than about harvest. But sometimes it is hard not to be discouraged. James recently prepared a presentation about Unlimited for the Bishop's Strategy Group as part of the consultation about becoming a BMO. On one of the slides James put up some of the names of young people we had written in our book after praying for them. Many of the names were unusual and spelt in unique ways and a few stuck in his mind. In the process we realised that we had probably prayed for more than 700 young people. Yet we only know the stories of a handful of them.

But tonight God gave us a glimpse of the seeds that He is sowing through us. While welcoming people into Soul Exeter we got talking to Nick, a youth worker, who told us the story of Siciliana. James recognised the unusual name and was instantly intrigued. Nick told him that for a few months now Siciliana had been attending one of the drop-in cafés that he runs in mid-Devon. A couple of months ago she had turned up as usual and seemingly out of nowhere asked if she could come to their church. They were amazed and delighted. She told them how she had been prayed for by Unlimited on the Cathedral Green and that she wanted to know more about God. Since that time she had been to church a few times and was in fact at Soul Exeter with him that night. It was encouraging to hear of the work that others are doing, to know that we are not alone.

But the story did not end there. At the end of the talk that evening, there was the chance for people to become Christians. A couple of young people responded. As the evening finished two girls went to talk to James to say that one of them had become a Christian. It was Siciliana. Small seed. Huge harvest.

## Monday 14th November 2011

We have a logo. It seems a small thing. An unnecessary distraction in all the more weightier things going on around us. But it isn't insignificant. The young people that we meet spend more and more time online. We can't ignore this fact. It is not my thing. I don't naturally turn to social media to share my every move, but they do, and we have committed to going to where they are, not expecting them to come to us. So we need an online presence, a website. We need an image and it needs to connect with them. Ed has started this process for us. We have a logo. It looks good to me!

## Thursday 1st December 2011

Today James became the leader of Unlimited Church. Just that. He remains a diocesan adviser but officially now has no other church responsibilities. No longer a parish vicar. The freedom is a privilege and we don't take it lightly.

## Saturday 3rd December 2011

Today has been humbling. We have so much to be thankful for. So many people give up their precious time to help us. Some of them hardly know us. Yet they came en masse to help us out. Because despite us spending every free moment at the house painting, scraping, washing, cleaning, the task is just too big and we cannot do it alone. We didn't ask for help. We are not good at that. One of James' colleagues knows that and so stepped in and took over. She filled our house with more than twenty people, all offering their time and skills. We had painters, carpenters, plasterers. So much was achieved. There is still much to do. But I no longer feel defeated. Their love and help has given us the boost and encouragement that we needed.

## Thursday 15th December 2011

I thought I was managing to hold it all together. Family, job, church, house painting. But the fact that my GP had to phone the national poisons unit this morning after I gave Toby the wrong dose of medicine makes me think I'm not quite as OK as I thought. Even as I gave him two dessertspoons full, I thought it was a strange amount. It took a while to even locate a dessertspoon. It was only Toby's questioning face that made me realise there was a problem. The considered opinion is that they think he will be OK, but that he needs to be kept under my supervision. So Toby ended up accompanying James and me to James' leaving assembly at the village school. It was nice for him to revisit old friends, to let him say goodbye as well. I have to confess to being mortified that he told everyone who would listen that he was there because Mummy had poisoned him.

## Saturday 24th December 2011

The help has continued to keep coming over December. My dad has painted many, many window frames. Unlike me he likes the gentle precision of this job. Steve and Helen have built a shed for us in the garden. Their only free time was at night so they were forced to work by the light of the street lamps over the wall. It was cold and raining when I guiltily left them, to pick up Josh and Toby. Countless others have painted, scrubbed, scraped and cleaned. The huge house has not been decorated for many years. However, we are going to move in four days' time and still we are not ready. We are not good at leaving jobs – if they don't get done in our initial flush of energy they are apt to get left for months. So we continue finishing up. The last thing I manage to fit in before we have to leave is painting the dining room picture rail. Even as I do it, I try to convince myself that I could leave it, that it doesn't matter. We are tired and we should go home and do something nice, something Christmassy. But I can't convince myself and I finish the painting before we close the door behind us, knowing that when we return it will be with all our boxes.

## Sunday 25th December 2011

We haven't made much of Christmas this year. Not in a worldly sense. No decorations. One big present each rather than multiple small ones (less packing). It is lovely. It is quiet. It is Christmas as perhaps it should be. Focused around what God did for us, and time with family. In church the wonder of Christmas hits me anew through the line of a song written by a friend: 'the word of God must learn to speak'.[22] Jesus gave up everything to come to earth as a baby. He came to live a life like just like ours. In the Gospel of John, Jesus is referred to as the Word of God, but when He chose to come to us as a baby, He couldn't even speak. As I ponder the enormity of this, I can't believe God chose to do that for us. But He came because He loves us and He knew He couldn't leave us. We needed Him, and He couldn't ignore that.

We put aside all that is about to change. All the hard work that has left us exhausted and drained, and we had a day as a family. With food and silly games. It was good.

---

[22] 'On Christmas Day' by Matt Osgood © Matt Osgood / RESOUNDworship.org, admin Jubilate Hymns Ltd. Used with permission.

# On the Move

*Wednesday 28th December 2011*

The vans arrived today. I say vans. This time we need three. Neither James nor I are good at getting rid of stuff, although we do try. For once it is probably a good thing, as even with three vans full of stuff we are going to rattle around in our new house. The men arrive early, and there is nothing particular for us to do at the start. There is much filling of boxes and they do not want us in the way. So I take the boys out into the lane. Josh wants to try to ride his new bicycle, his Christmas present. Toby decides this is the moment when he is going to learn to ride. Finally. They prove a great distraction and when we return breathless and pink-cheeked we find we are late. The first van has set off and we are needed in the new house immediately. We set off quickly without a second thought, intent on getting there in time to instruct the removals men. It is a good thing. There is no time to look back, to feel sad. We rush on to what lies ahead and only much, much later do we realise that we failed to say goodbye.

## Wednesday 4th January 2012

The house is strangely quiet. After the intense activity of the last week, all is silent. The boys are back at school. I feel guilty that they have returned tired and vaguely disorientated after their unusual holiday. James is at a meeting. For the first time I am alone in the house. It is good to be still. I am relieved that the move is done. That my brain can rest. It no longer has to worry endlessly over to-do lists, or arrange and rearrange virtual furniture. It is all done. We are moved. I will be still today. Tomorrow I will start the process of living in this house, in this city.

## Monday 9th January 2012

Another milestone. Another box ticked. Unlimited is legally a company. I am a company director along with James, Steve, Helen, Alison, Ruth, James and Ed. Eight of us to share this adventure.

## Thursday 12th January 2012

Tuesday evening has returned to our house. We are small enough (and the house is big enough) to fit around the dining room table. We have always wanted our Tuesday evening gathering to be based around a meal, around time spent sharing with others. Worship and teaching are key. But so is fellowship and friendship. For us friendship and food have always gone together. We like nothing better than inviting friends over for a meal. The lack of a kitchen at church has so far prevented us eating together on a Tuesday night, but now that we live a mere ten-minute walk from church, we can invite people to our house. Finally James' enormous table comes into its own. We didn't need it tonight. Tonight we were only small. We started with a meal, and after the boys went to bed turned to worship and the Bible.

It was a small start. But we have space to grow.

# Officially a Church

## Sunday 4th March 2012

Every event we have ever held in church contained food. I don't know if this will always be the case. But it is true so far. For me there is no easier way to draw people in, to show them quickly that they are loved and that they matter. Today we welcomed more people than ever into our church, as today was a day of celebration. After five years, today we were commissioned by the bishop to form a church. We are a BMO. A multigenerational church with a particular mission to youth. It was such a wonderful occasion. I think leadership (which is how we refer to ourselves, rather than directors) were worried how we would retain our casual, laid-back, accessible style with the formality of a bishop and several other visitors. But we need not have worried. They had come to celebrate with us who we are and what we are called to do. They came to encourage us, to spur us to continually seek after God and to assure us of their continued prayer. They did not want to change us.

The service was simple and powerful. I cried when Stacey sang over us. She was our first ever visitor to café and she still comes. Not every week now. But regularly enough. We have walked with her through some tough times and all of our interactions have been full of laughter and singing and cake. Angel cake still being her favourite. So how wonderful to have her to sing over us. It was not a traditional worship song. It was a pop song, but no less powerful or appropriate for that. I cried again when we all worshipped to another pop song which talked of us being free to dance and praise, with nothing holding us back. I'm surprised to find myself enjoying meeting God in songs where I hadn't been looking for Him before. I had polarised music into secular and sacred. Now these lines are blurring for me and I'm grateful for that. God is everywhere, all around us, and although I know that, music is helping me rediscover this truth anew. To hear a church full of young people singing, and meaning, words of freedom was amazingly powerful.

The strangest thing perhaps for me to come to terms with is that I now have the privilege of being a leader in the Church of England. In front of the church I signed my name beside James on the official documents. Rev James Grier (sacramental leader) and Dr Elizabeth Grier (leader). We are in this together. Our family mission has been recognised. It is both an honour and a responsibility.

Everyone at the service was given a link of broken chain to take home as a physical reminder of this day and that God offers to set us free from the stuff that shackles us. It will live in my pocket as a prompt to pray with thankfulness for what has been and hope for what has yet to come. It feels like an end and a beginning at the same time. An end to the uncertainty of who we are, and what we are doing. But we know that this is just the beginning. There is so much more to come.

## Wednesday 28th March 2012

We have now lived in the city for three months. I've almost got used to living opposite a pub and a supermarket. I don't know that I will ever get used to the sight of people sitting outside the pub drinking pints at 8am in the rush-hour fumes. The Friday and Saturday night noise of the city is so very different from the gentle lowing of the cows we used to have as our neighbours. I love being able to walk everywhere. Ironically I walk much more now that we live in the city. We walk to church, to the shops, to the cinema. We sometimes even walk to school. I thought village life would be healthy, but the reality was that everything but school was a car ride away. There was very limited public transport and, to our great sadness, no public footpaths.

Although we are getting used to our new life and it doesn't feel so new, we are still having people visit our house for the first time just to see where we are now. When they come, James and the boys love giving tours. Even the word 'tour' makes me cringe a little. It reminds me of long-ago school trips to vast historic houses. I think it bothers me because I am slightly embarrassed by how huge everything is. To us it feels like a very grand house. It is spread over three floors. We feel blessed and guilty. When we first moved in I really noticed that we were having to walk much further just to get around the house. Even simply cooking dinner takes more energy. I've read in magazines how everything in your kitchen should be within arm's reach, or at least organically organised. There is no way this is happening in our barn of a kitchen. I take five steps between kettle and sink, and another ten to the bin. And back again.

Unashamedly, however, I don't feel guilty about loving the bedroom. Our bedroom was once the drawing room of the house, the centre of the home, and I totally understand why life was lived in this room. It is magnificent, with a huge bay window and fireplace. Opposite the window are massive double doors that once connected into what is now Josh's bedroom. I'm very grateful that the diocese have sealed these shut, for our mutual privacy. In the bay window we have space for a sofa, chair and coffee table: an extra living space, as if the sofas downstairs in the living room, upstairs in the playroom and in James' study were not enough already. Our bedroom is so large that even with too many wardrobes (we are hoarders) and king-size bed there is ample room for this seating area. Seated there you are looking out at the garden at tree-top level. The tree closest to the window is a cherry, and today the blossom is breathtakingly beautiful, a white cloud that we are seemingly living in. On the boys' tour everyone's reaction to our bedroom is the same, a universal expression of delight in such a wonderful space. However, after the initial reaction, I've discovered I have two types of friends. Those who see the sofa as a 'gin and tonic sofa' – a place to have a drink while getting ready for an evening out, and those who see the sofa as an amazing, quiet space to sit and pray.

I think it should be both of those things. Gin and tonic and prayer. Although maybe not at the same time.

## Sunday 6th May 2012

Another half-marathon. I can hardly believe this is my third. But it has not been as joyful this time. My time remained stubbornly the same at two hours eight minutes despite a different, supposedly more effective, and certainly more expensive and strenuous gym regime. This time I ran alone. Since moving I have met up with Sarah twice a week to train on Tuesdays and Saturdays. But to add half an hour of driving before and after the running has changed the ease and accessibility. Everything needs to be planned. Other halves need to be consulted. More time is consumed. It hasn't worked and after this race I know that I will be back to training alone. After five years of sharing every step with my best friend, I don't know if I can face it, or be bothered to go on alone.

As much as I love living in the city the cost of moving has been high. I thought that half an hour's distance would not change much with my group of friends, but it has changed everything. I know in part things have changed as our children have grown; we have all taken jobs, picked up other activities. We had got into the habit of meeting together for Wednesday afternoon cakes, moving around the houses so that we all shared the burden of hosting. It used to be a highlight of my week. A midweek oasis. A place where I knew I would always be welcome. It was the place where I made friends. At other points of the week there were spontaneous cups of coffee after school drop-off. My friends are no longer doing this. They are not free either. But while I know in my head that what I am missing no longer exists, sometimes I can't help my heart resenting the fact that my husband's job, once again, has robbed me of something that was precious to me, and that I can't replace. In my head I know that this is a lie. It is not his job, but our calling, our church. But as much as my head knows that, today I feel sad. I feel alone.

## Thursday 31st May 2012

I'm not good at talking about sex. It's not actually how I would choose to spend a morning – talking about my sex life with twenty Year Ten children. Once again I found myself outside my comfort zone because James persuaded me that it was the right thing to do. No, more than that, he persuaded me that it would be great. That it would be absolutely fine.

We were working with a local charity that goes into schools to talk to children as part of a day focusing on love and marriage. The day enables students to consider various aspects of committed relationships and marriage by questioning a variety of local Christian couples. And the rules are there are no rules. They can ask absolutely anything they like. I was terrified. Would I blush? Would I understand their questions? Would they want to listen to me?

We spent an awkward hour in a coffee shop yesterday. We had been emailed a list of all the possible questions and we went out somewhere neutral to practise answering them. We wanted to physically voice what we would say to try to get the embarrassment over and done with. We were engrossed in the task, and only later realised that perhaps the conversation hadn't been entirely private. Another reason for tackling all the questions in advance is that we wanted to agree what we would and wouldn't say. To fix our boundaries, so that we were honouring one another. To my surprise, though, we both decided that we would answer every question as honestly as we could. The rules may be that they can ask absolutely anything, but you don't have to answer. But for us, we wanted to answer where we were able.

We were the youngest couple in school this morning. Therefore I think we possibly got a more direct set of questions. At first the students were so embarrassed. I don't think they really believed that they could ask anything. Then one loud-mouthed boy (it was always a boy), egged on by his mates, would get the ball rolling. Favourite position? How often? Where? Nothing too bad, or unexpected. In fact there was only one question all morning that we didn't answer, but that was because we didn't understand it rather than were unwilling. The surprise questions for me weren't about the sex, they were about the relationship, about us. Once they had got all the sex questions they could possibly think of out of the way, and the ice was well and truly broken, we started talking about what we regarded as the important stuff. We had a question about how we discipline our children. We talked about the fact that for us divorce is not an option, and rather than that meaning we are trapped, it means we are quicker to sort stuff out, to let go of grudges, because we will have to at some point, so we would rather just get on with it. We talked about how the relationship gets better over years, not that we get bored of each other. They were surprised that we were still friends, that we still talk, that we still have sex. We laughed with them. I found myself enjoying it. I hadn't considered before that my experience of marriage and relationship was worth sharing. But something valuable happened with these young people today.

## Sunday 3rd June 2012

Music has always been a part of my life. Before I was a Christian I knew something was happening when I played, not just messed around, but really played the harp with all my heart and all my mind. It centred me. It brought me back to wholeness, where life had fractured me. I was less argumentative, less difficult. I remember my mum commenting on this. Neither of us understood it then. But I do now. Music, worship, is where my soul connects with God and where I can begin to feel whole again.

So it is hard right now that worship is threatening to be something else. It can feel like a job, a chore, another thing to achieve. There are only two of us who lead worship in Unlimited at the moment. It feels as if I am always having to prepare a new set of worship. I don't want to let it become something that I resent, but I feel overwhelmed by the volume of worship that I have to prepare. I don't have the skills or the confidence just to rock up and go for it. I am a planner. I need to know that I have done my part of the job of leading worship to the best of my abilities. Then at that point I am happy to let go. To let God have His way, to break through, spontaneously shattering all my good intentions. I love it when that happens. I just feel duty-bound to prepare well in advance.

I don't find leading worship easy or natural. I'm much happier following someone else's lead. And over the years I have found it to be an unparalleled way of making a fool of myself. It is not uncommon for me to start a song and be totally unable to pitch the first note of the verse against the strummed chord. Or to play the wrong chords. Or, my most embarrassing ever moment was playing the modern version of a song while singing the old version of the tune. I didn't realise until afterwards what I was doing, despite it sounding a trifle odd, so I carried on regardless. In all these times I have had to remember that worship is for the audience of One. Actually the sound, the notes don't matter at all. What matters is my heart. As I make all these mistakes, which the perfectionist in me detests, I know what matters is not to give in to pride. If I start to get embarrassed I'm thinking more about me and my skills than I am about Jesus. What matters is to keep my heart fixed on Him. On what He thinks about me. Not what others think. So I have learned to laugh at myself and to keep my heart pure. But I still plan.

# Growing Up

*Sunday 17th June 2012*

Another first for Unlimited. Our first confirmation service. Again the bishop came to our church. Again we had to plan a service that honoured the values not only of our church, but also of the wider Church of England. We were so concerned about getting it right. We want to be unlimited by culture and tradition. We want young people to be themselves as they explore and express faith, rather than having to take on a form of church culture. We want to be real and relevant. But that has never meant to us that we should ignore the wealth of liturgy that is part of the Church of England. We are proud and honoured to be a part of the wider Church, and want to honour the whole Church in all that we do. There is so much that we can learn from the heritage of this organisation.

Tonight in our first-ever confirmation service it all came together. The old and the new. The traditional and the modern. We questioned everything that went into the service. Why were we including this song, that prayer? We planned and prayed over the service in a way that would be unsustainable for every Sunday service, but it was good to get this one right. Everything that went in had a meaning and a place. The younger members of the team didn't get it before tonight. They were dismissive of stuff that they saw as traditional and old-school. They did not understand why we put so much time into it, but the service really worked. Afterwards one of the team talked to me about how special the service had been and admitted that he had been wrong in his previous attitude. The ancient and modern melded beautifully together.

Tonight Jess and Katy stood before friends and family and declared their faith. Ed was confirmed as part of his journey to ordination in the Church. The service was a celebration of faith, of a living relationship with God. Families and friends gathered. A massive cream tea was served. The small church felt packed. Everyone felt at home – our visitors, our members, our young people. There was such a sense of the presence of God, and the knowledge that this was a holy moment.

## Friday 22nd June 2012

I have no words to say that could possibly comfort Josh and Toby today. Nothing I can say will change how they feel. I don't know how to meet them where they are. I feel the same. I know we should feel happy. Ed has finished his degree. His time at university has come to an end, and he is off. Headed for home and a summer of student exploits before he puts that life aside and starts working for a church, en route to ordination. We knew this day was coming. It is an exciting next step for him. But it is never good being the ones left behind. We have nothing new to focus on, to distract us. Unlike him. As I reflect on his time with Unlimited, there seems to be no area of church or family life where Ed has not made an impact. On Tuesday nights he will not be there to tell his terrible cheese-based jokes, to be the one who leaps up to help us clear away when others seemingly don't notice, to take an interest in Josh and Toby's day at school, to lead worship, to encourage us in prayer. He will not be there bringing energy on Wednesdays to the café team. The bedroom in our house that he occasionally stayed in, which is affectionately known as Ed's room, will have to go back to being called the spare room. He will not send out church Facebook posts or tweets. Without him I see only holes.

I'm not good at saying goodbye. God wants me to be a mother to this church. I love that. I love the people it is bringing into our lives. But letting them go again is harder than I ever imagined it could be. More than that, Ed leaving has forced me to confront a fear that I have been trying to bury, to pretend doesn't exist. Deep down I am afraid that no one will join the church. That no one will come to replace Ed. And if that is the case then what I am actually saying is that I am afraid that God isn't there for us. That God isn't going to follow through on His promises. But it has been good to recognise the place that I'd given this fear in my life because it has opened my eyes to see the effect that it has had on me. It has made me feel as though I need to screw my insides up tightly, to hold it all together. That I need to just carry on regardless, squash down the fear, not even acknowledge it. But holding it together is exhausting, and Ed leaving has brought me to the end of the road. I can't go on like this.

So today I am going to choose to trust God. Trust that He will be faithful to His promises. I pray and recognise the fear I have been burying. I repent of believing it and allow God to bring peace in its place. Now instead of feeling as if my insides are clenched, desperately holding everything together, I feel more like Indiana Jones in the *Last Crusade*. In his final challenge in the quest to reach the Holy Grail he has to cross a path that he cannot see. He has to step out in faith, and it is almost as if when he does, the path rises up to meet him. That is how I now feel. I can't see the path ahead. But I know that it is there. Now that fear is not holding me back I feel free to step out.

## Saturday 28th July 2012

I don't often enjoy being proved wrong, but I did today. In my blinkered thinking I've always thought that students shouldn't get married. They're too young. They should wait until they have finished their degrees. They should live their student life to the full. Today I was proved joyously and wonderfully wrong at the wedding of Pete and Rachel. Although we haven't persuaded them to come to Unlimited yet (we keep asking!), we have known them since moving to Devon. Their journey to this day was not what either of them expected. They have had to face stuff so difficult that I cannot even begin to imagine their pain. Honestly, I don't even want to. And yet through the worst of times their love held and seemingly got stronger and sweeter. They have turned to each other and God and have such a joy and a happiness in each other, in their friends, in this day, that I don't think I have felt at any other wedding. This is no naïve couple getting married during university because they don't want to wait a moment longer. This is a couple whose love has been forged in a furnace and has come out as pure as gold and as strong as titanium. I am amazed that the last few years not only have not crushed them but have also been a place where they have grown and flourished. Not every couple would have survived. I was honoured to be a guest. I am delighted to be proved wrong.

## Friday 3rd August 2012

When you've waited so long for a day to arrive, you can feel nervous when it finally does. There is the fear that it will not live up to expectations. That it may all be a huge let-down. Or the reverse. Everything is so amazing you never want it to end. You frantically try to record every detail in your mind so that you will not forget a single thing. I have been waiting for today for seven years. James totally does not understand my excitement. He is going along with this trip to London because it is so important to me, but I know he would be just as happy back home. He would not even bother to watch the Olympics on the TV but, for my sake, we have bought tickets and transported the family to London. Just so that we can say, and our children can say, that we were there. We were part of this great thing where nationality, race, religion all ceased to matter. All that mattered was people striving to be the very best that they could be. To run the races set before them the very best they could. To see humanity excel. To me it feels like a physical outworking of all that we long to see spiritually for the people in our church.

We had wanted tickets to the main arena, to the velodrome or possibly to the swimming. After our abject failure to get tickets of any description in the first round we were grateful for any at all, even if we knew nothing about hockey. With very limited hockey knowledge, we planned a family trip to London with a trip to the Olympics as the highlight. The tickets gained us entry to the Olympic Park, and we arrived to see, on the big screen, Britain winning their first gold medal for rowing. The medals kept on coming for the whole day. The atmosphere in the park was joyous. Our visit to London 2012 was everything I had hoped for. A national celebration. Something never to forget. To be proud that I was there. That we were a part of it.

But there was a flip side to the day for me. Although today was everything I had hoped for, I have also been aware of a well of unspoken sadness within me. For all the joy that these events are bringing, I can't separate the games with how, for me, it all started. London was announced as the 2012 Olympic host on 6th July 2005, at 12.49pm. I was in the kitchen in Birmingham giving the boys their lunch, as I was every day at that time. I had the radio on. I was eagerly anticipating the announcement. I was hoping the Olympic committee would choose London and not Paris against popular predictions. The boys did not understand what was happening when lunch was suddenly interrupted by Mum going slightly crazy, but they joined in the dancing and the cheering and we whooped around the kitchen in utter joy. It was a historic moment of news, and it was good. Just twenty-four hours later we sat in the kitchen in shock. We weren't silent. Life is never silent with a three- and a one-year-old, but even they picked up my horror as I heard of the events of the terror attack unfolding in London that day. I was sickened that in such a short space of time our world could change from feeling so utterly joyful to being so full of sadness. I couldn't make sense of it myself. I could not even begin to make sense of it for my children. So we had lunch and carried on. But there was no dancing that day.

## Monday 6th August 2012

Our first Unlimited wedding! Mr and Mrs West. Ruth has married James. A wonderful day of celebration. Honestly, as a couple, I am a little in awe of them. Ruth is as beautiful as James is handsome. Between them they seem to be able to do absolutely anything. As a couple they will be unstoppable. They are outgoing, sporty, clever, adventurous. I'm surprised their honeymoon is not climbing Kilimanjaro or kayaking down the Amazon. I know that married life is often talked about as a great adventure, but for this couple I think it will be absolutely true in every sense of the word. More importantly than all of that, their hearts are chasing after God's own heart, they love the young people of our church, they know how to have fun, they are kind and generous with their time and their gifts. They are a blessing to Unlimited.

## Thursday 9th August 2012

I delight when new people join Unlimited, but finally I have reached the point where I don't actually *need* them to. I feel free from the worry and the fear that people will not come. I'm free to strengthen and nourish, protect and mother the church. As I am called to do. But I don't need to worry. I don't need to fear. That isn't my job. At the moment I find myself returning again and again to a conversation that Jesus had with Peter.[23] Three times Jesus asks Peter, 'Do you love me?' Three times Peter replies, 'Yes' and Jesus commands him, 'Feed my sheep.' Three times Peter is asked. Three times he replies with a heartfelt, 'Yes'. I know theologians have discussed this passage at length, but I think the point that God wants to make for me is incredibly simple. If you love Me, then feed My sheep. He asks three times because this isn't always as easy as it sounds. We can find ourselves with many questions in between Jesus' question, 'Do you love Me?' and the subsequent reply, 'Feed My sheep'. We can find ourselves saying 'I do, but ...', or 'yes, what about ... ' But for me, and for Peter, it boils down to the simple fact that if we love Jesus we will feed His sheep. With all our questions, all the things we don't understand, in the end it is that simple. Not easy, but simple.

## Monday 13th August 2012

Our little group has been at Soul Survivor for four days. They have survived the heat, the rain, the flooding, the

---

[23] John 21:15-19.

camping, the cooking, the showers. More than surviving, they appear to be flourishing. Long forgotten is the awkwardness of the first day when the tents were up, possessions were arranged, but there was nothing more to do. I could see some of the young people who'd never experienced anything like this before wondering what on earth they were doing in this slightly muddy field making polite conversation with people they hardly knew. There were only so many ways to explain to them that they needed to be patient before they passed judgement on this festival. We tried explaining that the event kicks off with a main meeting at 7pm and after that all the fun starts. They didn't look like they believed us, but they get it now. They are having the time of their life. A high point of their summer.

I too am having a good time. It is so good to be here with the young people but I can't pretend I'm only here for them. I'm here for me too. Over the years I've had so many people ask me if I don't feel too old for Soul Survivor, if I don't find the teaching repetitive, or too young? My answer to that has always been 'no'. Personally I've always found that there is something new to learn if we have teachable hearts. This year I have been struck afresh by the story of Rachel and Leah.[24] It's not a new story to me, but I found myself looking at it with new eyes. Both women are married to Jacob. Rachel had Jacob's love but wanted his children. Leah had his children, but longed for his love. There is a complicated outworking of these facts in their story, but this is what it boils down to. Each one wants what the other one has. Their story is not one of happiness.

[24] Genesis 29:16-30:24.

So many of the young girls that I talk to are caught in this endless cycle. They spend so much time looking around at what others have and wanting and hoping for that. They think that everyone else is doing better than they are; they are having more fun, they are thinner, more beautiful, cleverer. They are exhausting themselves with comparisons, and they literally can't escape. In this world of social media 24/7 they are bombarded with the highlights of their friends' lives, and see their own as lacking. The story of Rachel and Leah inspires me afresh with the vision of our church. That we will see young people coming to know and pursue the life that God has given them. In the words taken from Hebrews 12:1-2, that they will run the race set before them. Their race, their life. Not anyone else's. We want them to know that God has created them as special and unique, that they need to stop wishing they were more like someone else and need to start loving themselves, just the way they are. Just as God does.

## Monday 3rd September 2012

We have an intern! An amazing guy called Jack has come to work with us for the year. From a chance conversation I had over a cup of coffee in March we have got to this point. We can't pay him anything. We are offering him theological training of sorts, and his bus fare. That's all. Anything extra he is earning with his job in a café. It will only give him pocket money. He is full of enthusiasm and new ideas. Fresh energy and vision. There will be times when he can't get the bus home, when we finish too late and the journey is too far. Then he is coming to stay with us. I'm not sure about sharing my space. It blurs my boundaries between work and family. I'm not sure I will be very hospitable, at all hours of the day and night, but I want to be. I want him to feel welcome. I want him to feel at home with us.

# Kit Kat Sundays

## Sunday 9th September 2012

Even when you have a vision to do church that is unlimited by tradition, it can be hard to recognise it when it looks nothing like you were expecting. You begin to realise that you are indeed limited by tradition. Before we started on this journey, if you had asked me to describe what going to church was, I would have painted a picture of people meeting together in a building. Their time together would involve worship, teaching and prayer. I may even have said that this usually happens on a Sunday. I was perfectly happy that there are a myriad of ways for this to look and feel. But I did think that church would contain all of those elements. I love the fact that everybody is different, unique. We each have our own ways of connecting with God. We all obey the command from Hebrews that we should 'not [give] up meeting together'[25] in our own way. And God loves all of His Church. Every expression.

---

[25] Hebrews 10:25.

But for church not to be in a building, not to involve worship and teaching and prayer. Is that still church? Is the people of God meeting together in His name enough? I'm surprised to find myself saying that yes it is enough, because that is what we've been exploring. We have come to realise that church doesn't have to look the same every time we meet together. Each Sunday of the month has a different focus, but the Sunday following Soul Exeter is probably when we look least like a 'church' to a traditional mindset. Soul Exeter is now run mainly by a team from Unlimited Church. Soul Exeter still provides young people with a monthly mini-taste of Soul Survivor throughout the year, with a focus on worship, teaching and ministry. Changing the service on the Sunday that follows Soul Exeter was partly a practical decision forced upon us by the worship team. We just didn't have enough people to run Soul Exeter and a service that looked like 'church' on a Sunday. But it was also a dawning realisation that we are called to be unlimited by culture and tradition. If we had met together for worship, teaching and prayer on a Saturday, why were we doing it all over again on a Sunday? So we have started to try something different where we get together as the people of God, as a church, but where we don't have to do anything that looks like 'church'.

Today we went kayaking. We are calling this Sunday Kit Kat Sunday. A Sunday when we take a break from church, together. There was much laughter, and plenty of splashing. Young people joined us who at the moment would not even consider coming into a church building for a service. They came because they seem to like hanging out with us. Put simply, they like us. We love them. We had great fun. They came a step closer to God. They began to see that 'church' is not what they had thought. We began to see that church is so much more than a building, worship, teaching and prayer. It is people. It is the living body of Christ doing life together.

## Saturday 6th October 2012

Today people paid to hear me play the harp. Walked in off the street to listen to me. No, that is not strictly true. They came to listen to Emma and me performing together, as equals. Harpe Noire we have called ourselves, as we both play black harps. We are both teachers. At present I have only a very few pupils, but they were all there. The pressure of not letting them down was huge. I was so nervous. It was so long since I had done anything like this I was not sure what to expect. I was shocked to see my hands physically shaking as I readied myself for the first piece. My hands were clammy and my voice did not sound like my own. At the first mistake (there were many – hopefully hidden) there was a surge of adrenaline that sharpened my senses and focused me with a new intensity. I was equally delighted and disappointed when the end came. Half of me was sagging with relief and the other half of me wanted the feeling to last forever. I'm hooked. I love working as a harpist. Weddings, concerts, teaching. I might have to start being brave and admit to being a harpist when people ask what I do.

# Unlimited Goes Large

*Sunday 4th November 2012*

We have been aware for a while that Mary Arches Church, our location, our base, is not always easy to find. We joke that our description of the location of church is determined by the age of the people we are talking to. We choose the shops that we use to direct them according to their age and stage in life. For the truly younger generation we don't even mention the shops, but locate it in relation to the nightclubs. It is good to see the dawning recognition in people's eyes when we have hit upon the right set of directions, but it remains a fact that we are hard to find. Unless we physically invite a young person, they are not going to stumble across us. We can offer to show them where we are, but often quite rightly, they don't always want to accompany a stranger across the city to an unknown location.

But for the last three days we have changed all of that. Instead of young people coming to us, we went to them. We put up a marquee on the Cathedral Green, located the cunningly hidden plugs (in the wall, no less!) for our tea urn, picked up the beanbags and took café out of the building. We had a double-decker bus full of games consoles parked outside the cathedral. A volleyball net and a football cage were located on the grass. We talked, prayed, played, ate cake, listened, laughed. The Green is always busy with young people when the weather is good, but this was something special. There was a buzz. People wanted to know who we were, what we were doing. We were happy to tell them that, but much more so to tell them why we were doing it. Why we were giving up our free time on chilly November days to hang around in the open air. We wanted to tell them of the God who knows them, and loves them, and is longing for relationship with them. And many people were happy to listen.

Friday and Saturday nights were spent in Mary Arches Church. We wanted the young people to know where to find us when we are not on the Green, and we were pleased so many came along. On Saturday there was a big finish to the event with food, fun and laughter. On Friday night we opened up church for an open mic event. It was good to see the building alive with youth. They were genuinely interested in learning more about the God they've never met, but can see living in the people of this church. Of all those that we met over the three days, Kyle stands out to me. He is a real presence in the room. No mistaking when he is around. He always wears a hat, is very fashion conscious and is an amazing dancer. I could be intimidated, but there is something so incredibly genuine about him. He talks tough, but he also wants to listen. He has come to café every day we have been on the Green. He is intrigued by us. He came into church this evening and later said to one of the team that he feels safe in here, when he doesn't have any other safe places in his week. To hear this makes sense of all that we do. Makes sense of all the time, energy and love that we pour into this church. Whatever happens after this mission of taking Unlimited out of the building and on to the Green, it will have been worth it just for that one comment.

## Tuesday 6th November 2012

I didn't quite know what to do with myself today after picking up the boys from school. I didn't have to cook and serve a meal for fourteen tonight. I didn't have to juggle the demands of homework, music practice and table setting. I did not have to squeeze too many people around the table I once thought was huge, but which I now have to reluctantly admit is too small for our purposes. Instead from this point forward on a Tuesday night we will go to Mary Arches to eat dinner, our family being just a part of the larger church family of Unlimited.

I'm both excited and saddened by this move. It was our great joy when we moved into the city to welcome the whole church into our house for a meal on a Tuesday night before we turned to study, prayer and worship. We always knew that fourteen would be our limit. Beyond that we would not be able to sit together at the table to eat. We would not be able to fit comfortably, or even squash uncomfortably, into the living room after the meal. It is wonderful that there are now too many of us to fit into our house, but I think we all missed the familiar comfort, and warmth, of our home. The church felt like a huge, empty space. Not everyone was sure that they liked the change. It reminded me of when we moved the café out from the back room and into the main body of Mary Arches. It wasn't a popular move. It didn't feel comfortable. But it was the right thing to do. It allowed us to grow. And so in time I know that we will all again get used to the new routine, how to cook without a kitchen, how to serve everyone and make sure they all feel as welcomed and included as they would if they were invited into our house. This move will give us space to grow.

Tonight fifteen of us gathered. As we have done since we moved into the city, we started the Tuesday evening by eating together. There is no kitchen, but with a hotplate and rice cooker situated on a table in the back corridor, James and Jack served us all a delicious curry. Even though it is not in a home, our vision is still that it will be a place where we will sit and talk. Where we will try not to dash off, racing to the next job, and the next. Perhaps, hardest of all, we will try not to be on our phones. To not take refuge from the awkward silences by checking social media or email. And it won't always be easy. We don't know each other all that well and conversation will not always flow. But if we do not take this time out together, intentionally sit and eat as family, then maybe we never will. All too easily we fall into the pattern of forming friendships with like-minded people, and making passing acquaintances of others. Some people we will never speak to. But this way, while we are still small, we will all get to know each other.

It will be awkward at times. It may feel forced. But then, family isn't always easy.

We followed the meal with teaching. It is a challenge to meet the needs of our church. Some have been Christians a matter of days. Others have known and loved Jesus for nearly fifty years. We have neither the space nor the people to teach in separate streams. Nor do we want to. We want to be inclusive. Instead, James talked to us all. He has a way of taking the Bible and bringing it to life. To make it make sense. To help us see what we haven't before. I know I'm biased, but I always learn something new from him. Even when I think I know the topic he will bring a fresh understanding. So, old and new, we all listen together. After that we separated into groups. James and I had tried to be cool and with-it, so we named the groups Twitter, Facebook and Wikipedia. The names didn't go down well. Apparently we were trying too hard, but I think they understood what we were meaning by the labels. The groups all discussed the teaching and the personal response. But the idea was that each group went into it with a different approach. Twitter in bite-sized chunks, Wikipedia in greater depth, Facebook somewhere in-between. I'm not sure it worked out that way. I didn't feel as though I learned less or had been short-changed from joining the Twitter group.

Tonight was just a start. A tester for how we can go deeper together as a church with such a diverse grouping. We are truly multigenerational. We are at every age and stage. Nobody really has a peer that they can befriend. Nobody has a life that looks like theirs. So we have to be friends to all. Love everyone. Live together. Learn together.

## Wednesday 7th November 2012

Café was full today. It was filled with some of the large number of young people that we met last week out on the Green. Although many of them had come to the open mic night, a few had never been in a church building before. When I was chatting to them I learned that they mostly had a stereotype of what they thought a church would be like. What would be allowed. Many expected silence, candles, pews and organ music. I love the fact that we are not the stereotype that they are expecting. Inside the church was bright, warm and inviting. Many hot chocolate mountains and cakes were served. It feels like the start of a new season for café.

## Monday 19th November 2012

No school is perfect. I know that, but sadly we have had to face the fact that Toby is not at the right school. It's also time to choose a senior school for Josh. It is all change again for them both. They hate change, and we hate doing it to them. It feels like they have only just settled in, stopped being the new boys, and we are having to look to the next move. We were not expecting to be in this position after only a year, but actually the writing has been on the wall from almost the day that they started at St Margaret's. Their blazers were still stiff and new, their shoes unscuffed when James and I were called into the headmistress' office. Naively I had thought this was the norm. A welcome and 'how are you getting on' that was extended to all new parents. It wasn't that meeting at all.

When they had started just over a year ago, Josh in Year Five, Toby in Year Three, there had been very few boys in the junior school. No, it was worse than very few. In fact, Josh was the only boy in his class. Toby was one of just three. The gender balance was so awry because, although the junior school was technically co-educational, the senior school only accepted girls and so the majority of boys chose to leave well in advance of Year Six, going to schools that offered them both a junior and senior option. But this was all about to change. In an attempt to boost dwindling school numbers, the governors had decided that the senior school too was to become co-educational and it was Josh's school year that would be the first to accept boys in the senior school. The bottom line was that the school needed more pupils. Class sizes were becoming too small and the school was looking increasingly unviable financially. The governors knew this was a long-term solution, but they hoped that offering schooling all the way to the age of eighteen would persuade boys to remain. At the same time Josh and Toby were actively recruited into the junior school in the hope that it would encourage others to follow suit. Trailblazers, we thought.

Many people thought we were naïve or crazy. They were more than surprised that we were sending the boys to what they thought was a girls' school. But it felt like the right school. We knew it would take time to go fully co-educational, and we knew it wasn't perfect. However, from their village school of seventy pupils, this school seemed the right fit. It was small and caring, where children were treated as individuals and encouraged to be the best that they could be. And so they had joined, albeit with our reservations.

But at the meeting with the headmistress, rather than the welcome I was expecting, we were informed that the governors had now decided against the senior school going co-educational. The news came as a total shock. We were told they were welcome to stay for their junior school years, but no longer.

My immediate concern was about breaking the news to Josh. It had been his decision to leave Rockbeare village school to start Year Five in a new school. But all along he had been very clear that he was only going to move school once. He has never liked change. It unsettles him and he would much rather that everything stayed the same. We did give him the option to stay until the end of Year Six and then move to senior school along with his current set of friends. But he knew that would mean a lot of driving. A lot of sitting in the car. A lot of wasted time. So he was brave. He chose to move to St Margaret's, knowing that from there he could continue into senior school. He would never have to change school again. When we had to tell him of the headmistress' decision he was angry and upset, but now I think he is relieved that he will be going somewhere new. It's not that he is unhappy as such. It's just that he is the only boy in a class of twelve girls, and that is not an easy place for a ten-year-old boy to be. In a sweeping generalisation, boys seem much simpler than girls. Boys get cross, they thump each other, they forget, they move on. Girls, we are finding, are so much more difficult to understand. They can be mean and fickle and oh-so-brutal with their words. In this world of girls, Josh has learned to think of himself as being a bit like Switzerland. Neutral in friendship disputes, known not to take sides, but a good person to confide in, friend to all. I am proud of how he is, but I wish with all my heart that things were different. He is Switzerland because he cannot have a best friend, as everyone else does. Whenever he is seen to have a friendship with one girl more than any other, both are teased mercilessly. Teased until any fledgling friendship is abandoned. The girl returns to her former friends. Josh is once again alone. I ache for his loneliness. There is nothing I can do for him.

It is the same for Toby. He started the school year with three boys in his class, but one by one they have all left for other schools. He has another two years left of junior school and I would not unsettle him needlessly, but we have to face the fact that this is not the right school for him either. So we will start looking at our options, hoping that the way ahead will be clear.

## Wednesday 21st November 2012

We have two new members of church. Well, they are not new, but they are newly 'official', I guess. As part of our company structure we elected to have directors and members. Anyone who is willing to make a public declaration that they belong to our church and commit to our key principles can become a member. The directors are elected from and by the membership. For the first time we have members who are not directors. More people are beginning to come. Others will follow. But for now our membership makes it into double figures.

## Friday 30th November 2012

I'm so hurt tonight. The pain is almost physical and I just want to sit and hold myself together. Over months I have offered friendship and love to a guy who joined our church. We have welcomed and accepted him. Today it feels like everything we have ever done, thought or felt has been thrown back at us. He seems not to realise that, as well as being leaders, we are people. We are ordinary people who will get stuff wrong. But hopefully will also say sorry. We are people like anybody else who feel hurt when hurtful things are said to us, and about us. It's made me question more deeply what the cost of leadership really is. I've always known that being constantly questioned and also maybe feeling constantly judged is part of the package. I say judged because sometimes when people question if the church is doing well, or whether they like the worship, the style, the welcome, it can feel personal. As though they are judging us and all that we do. I do try to welcome the fact that it has to be OK for people to question us and what we are doing. I try to be open to well-meaning criticism and not to take it personally. But tonight, with this guy, it does not feel OK. It hurts. I feel betrayed. We have been challenged at every level. In his eyes we are getting it very wrong. He chose to tell us exactly how he felt.

I sometimes think that being in church leadership is a bit like being project leader on *The Apprentice*. It is much safer in the early rounds of this reality TV show simply to be one of the team. To stand up as leader is a risk. It can all go wrong. A lot is expected of you. Tonight it feels like our leadership has gone wrong and that honestly it would have been much safer just to be one of the team. I regret taking a risk instead of the safer, easier path. So I sit with God and it hurts. I share my pain. Some of what was said about us today was right. There was truth in it. But not all of it. And as I sit God starts to heal that pain, but also show me more about leadership. To help me look more deeply at this calling that sometimes I feel I've accidentally fallen into.

God shows me that my position is not like being on *The Apprentice*. Leadership within Unlimited is not something that I've ever grasped or sought after. It's more like a gift that He has given to me. As I sit for longer I also begin to realise that for years, as I've been reading commands to leaders in the Bible, I've been reading them with a threatening kind of soundtrack going on in my head. I've heard 'a lot is expected', 'set a good example', 'have a well-behaved family'[26] as stern instructions with Darth Vader-type music playing menacingly behind. I have measured myself against these words to see where I'm failing. As I sat with God tonight He changed the accompanying soundtrack. These words are not Him telling me off. They are Him encouraging me to be the best that I can be. They are supposed to be inspirational to me. He is certainly being kind. God knows that to lead like this, to be like this, is my heart's desire. He also knows that I won't achieve it, I won't hit the mark on everything. But He still wants me to live to be the very best that I can be. He doesn't want to settle for mediocrity. Nor do I.

---

[26] See Titus 1:6-9.

# I Can't Believe It's
# Not Midnight

## Monday 24th December 2012

Our first Christmas as a church. Many of our young people don't live with families that go to church and so a service on Christmas Day would be inaccessible to them. It just would not be understood if they wanted to go away from the family for any part of the day. So instead we are having our main celebration on Christmas Eve. Not even over midnight, but at 10pm so they can catch buses home. We chuckle over the name we've chosen – 'I can't believe it's not midnight'. Probably we're trying too hard, but we don't mind! Tomorrow those that can will gather in our house for breakfast and communion, but tonight is where the whole church gather and celebrate together. We sing carols, we read the Bible, we watch a video clip or two. It is simple, stripped back and wonderful. There is space and silence to wonder anew at the enormity of what Jesus did for us by stepping down to earth. Humbling Himself for us. Celebrating Christmas with young people who have never before seen this meaning or understood this part of the story, have never looked beyond the trappings of presents, food and drink is amazing. We return home with hearts full.

We then have to wait for very excited children to go to sleep. They have never stayed up this late and dire threats that Father Christmas is waiting and is getting impatient are to no avail. Regardless of the late hour we know they will be up again at 6am. It promises to be a short night.

## Friday 25th January 2013

Today has been a strange day. A day where we have become so aware of God's guiding in our life. We asked that the way ahead for the boys' schooling would be clear, but honestly, when at 11am we accepted places for Josh and Toby at Exeter School, we were still not sure we were doing the right thing. The plan is for them to start in September. Josh in the senior school, Toby in the junior. Once more we have promised that they won't have to move school again. This time we are as sure as we can be that they can stay until they are eighteen. It seemed like the right next step, ignoring the fact that even with generous bursaries we don't know exactly how we are going to afford it.

Then at the end of what was just a normal day at their current school, parents and teachers were informed that the school would be closing at the end of the summer term. The official announcement to the press will be made on Monday. It has gone bankrupt. Suddenly 200 children, or, more correctly, 200 sets of parents were desperately trying to find new schools. The upset and panic is terrible. Many parents have missed the school application window. Most schools have allocated 2013 places. All parents can do is wait and see. Pupils and parents are distraught at the school closing, the mismanagement that has brought them to this place, the way they were informed, the teachers being made redundant. There are tears and anger and harsh words and a very deep sadness. I can see all the emotion. I can empathise with the pain and the panic. But we are not a part of it. We are protected from it, and for that I am so, so grateful.

## Sunday 3rd February 2013

A legal requirement of a company is that we have a meeting every year for the members. Formally we need to present the accounts and vote on new directors. This is what we need to do but we are free to choose how we do it. So we chose to have a party. An excuse to get together, to have fun, to celebrate the year that has gone and to look forward to the next year. To have our eyes lifted up again to our vision. To be refreshed and encouraged. It is good to stop and celebrate. It is too easy to look ahead for the next thing without being properly grateful for all that has gone before. So we stopped this afternoon. We had a party and we celebrated this new church.

It was lovely that Chris and Sarah came to the party to hear our fresh vision for the year. It was good to meet them. I've heard all about them, but this was my first meeting in person. Up until today all I knew about them was that Chris was the non-church-member keen enough to attend our 6.30am Wednesday morning prayer meetings and

Sarah was his fiancée who didn't even live in Devon. I've never met Chris as I don't attend early morning prayer because I am getting the boys ready for school. In fact, very few of our church members manage to get to this early morning meeting, so I was aware that something about this guy must be pretty exceptional. He and Sarah are thinking about joining Unlimited after they are married. However, wherever they choose to go to church, Sarah wants them to start together, to make friends together. For it to be their church, rather than Chris' church that Sarah joins at a later point.

This afternoon they came to the party to meet us as a church, to hear about both what we are celebrating from the past year and what we are looking forward to in the year to come. To decide if we were the right church. Apparently they liked us and thankfully it confirmed what they were already thinking. They will come to Sunday gatherings together in the autumn, and until then Chris will continue to pray for the life of the church early on a Wednesday. I am amazed at his commitment. Personally I might just have waited until after I got married to start at a new church. But not Chris. While patiently waiting and honouring Sarah's wishes, he will be wholeheartedly a part of Unlimited. He is determined to pray for the church, and all that we do, while he prepares to get married. I can sense that both Chris and Sarah will be an exciting addition to the church. It is easy to see that they are both passionate and committed, and looking forward to when they can join us fully. But they are so much more than that. They are fun and young, and they bring energy and vitality and encouragement to the church. We will be very blessed by them.

The story of how Chris and Sarah came to Unlimited is another reminder to me that we just need to trust God. He has promised us people. Any ideas we would come up with to find new people to join would not have found us Chris and Sarah. They are brought to us by God. Last month James went to an evening meeting. Nothing unusual in that. But I remember being surprised at his quick return. He had been out for less than an hour. He was embarrassed to admit to me that he had gone to the meeting on the wrong night. He didn't really know why he'd done it, the meeting was correctly entered in his diary. It turned out that his trip was not wasted. At the house where the meeting should have been he had met a guy lodging there and they had arranged to go for a beer later in the week. Chris was new to Exeter, getting married later in the year, and trying to find a church to join with his fiancée. They hadn't considered Unlimited but there was an instant, obvious camaraderie between James and Chris. After a beer and a chat there was a fledgling friendship. We were so excited when Chris later told James that he and Sarah were thinking about joining us after their wedding.

## Monday 4th February 2013

It's not about numbers. We know that by now. Which makes it feel even stranger that we feel called to pray this year for our membership to expand to forty. Currently we have just over twenty members. I am excited about what a church of forty would look like, what we could do. I'm scared, too, to step out in prayer in case God doesn't answer. How will we feel if after a year we are nowhere near a membership of forty? What if we have totally misheard God on this, will it call into question everything else? It would be easier and safer to stay as we are, going along in relative safety, not stepping out. But even as I think that I know that I am limiting myself and God in an attempt to protect myself, and all that will achieve is to water down my faith and relationship with God into something tame, nowhere near the life-changing transformational freedom that He promises. We are called to be unlimited in our openness and expectation of God. Here is the moment for me to live that out in faith. I will pray for forty.

## Saturday 9th February 2013

The boiler at church has broken. Thankfully not for the heating. That boiler is still working despite being incredibly noisy and inefficient. The boiler that has broken was providing us with all our hot water. Cooking for Tuesday nights has become even more difficult. It was already a challenge. With no kitchen to speak of, and larger numbers to cater for, the cooking has moved out of the back corridor and is now being done in the main body of the church. A makeshift kitchen is erected each week, assembled from a collapsible table, two single halogen rings and a rice cooker. After eating the kitchen is cleared away, every item has to be carried to where it is stored. The church is then transformed from dining room to an area where we can worship, learn and talk. The final job is the washing-up. Beyond the back room along a single-file corridor there is a sink, a kitchen cupboard and a fridge.

This is where the washing-up happens. Unless of course someone needs the toilet. Because beyond the kitchen area, if you squeeze past all the washers-up, is the one toilet. Sound is not protected between toilet and kitchen. There is no privacy. It is not at all ideal. And without hot water on tap, the task of washing-up has become even worse. Now a multitude of kettles provide scalding water, very slowly.

I had thought the obvious solution was to get the boiler fixed, and quickly. But James has other ideas. He is wondering if this is the right moment to think about changing a few things. We love Mary Arches Church. The building, the space, the location. But inside it is not ideal. One toilet is not sufficient, and its location is at best awkward, at worst embarrassing. He is wondering if we should consider an extra toilet, and changing the kitchen layout so that it could be a place to cook. He's right, of course. We will have to think about what we can afford.

# Another
# Perspective

## Thursday 21st February 2013

I can't sleep tonight. I've tried and given up. I hope the boys are managing to sleep better than I am. I could blame the mattress, or the unfamiliar sounds outside, or the hot airlessness, but in truth it is none of those things. It is more that I'm nervous. We're in a strange house in a village in Africa. We've been waiting for this moment for months, but now that we're here I feel incredibly unsure about everything. Why have we done this? We could have just gone on holiday. Maybe we *should* just have gone on holiday. Are we as a family up to this? Do we have anything of value to offer?

This is our second visit to Africa but probably the only trip Josh and Toby will remember. It seems such a long time since we were last able to visit James' sister. She lives in Cape Town with her husband and boys and we miss them all keenly. We have long wanted to return to visit them, but have been waiting until Toby was eight, the age that you officially become old enough to go on safari. Over time in our minds it has built up into being a holiday of a lifetime, but we have also always known that we wanted the holiday to be more than that. We wanted the boys to experience more of the world than tourist attractions. For them to return talking and thinking about more than safari and shooting (with cameras) the big five.[27]

Our day started with a dawn trip up Table Mountain. It ends sleeping (or not) in the purple house on the staff cluster of LIV village.[28] We knew relatively little about LIV village before we arrived at Durban airport. We had heard Tich and Joan Smith speak at a Soul Survivor festival of their vision of a village for orphaned and vulnerable children, where each child had a home, a family and a mother. Where their hope for each child was to rescue them, restore their life, raise them as a leader and release them as a star. We were inspired and intrigued by this vision, and wanted to know more. So we are here for five days. After being collected from the airport we drove out to the village. As we entered I was struck by the clusters of brightly coloured houses. It looked a place so full of hope, of love. Inside our house we found the same to be true. Everything is done to the very highest standard, there is no making-do. Everything is the best that it can be. These children matter, and everything in their environment shows that they are valuable, from the beds, to the

---

[27] The 'big five' is a term originally used by game hunters for the five hardest animals to shoot – lion, leopard, rhinoceros, elephant and buffalo.

[28] See www.liv-village.com (accessed 19th March 2018).

bedding, to the kitchen fittings, to the cushions in the living area. I had worried about what we were going to eat. We were self-catering but I had nothing with me apart from a few rusks. I was humbled to find a fridge full of food. But it was not just any food. It was amazing food. Food that we would only rarely treat ourselves to. We will be eating better than we eat at home. The local branch of a national upmarket supermarket gives them their food as it approaches the sell-by date, and they gratefully accept. I find sushi, prawns, papaya, watermelon. More food than we could possibly eat. And they have filled our fridge to welcome us. I feel guilty. They deserve this food, not us.

But even with a fridge full of food I do not need to cook. As soon as we have dropped our bags Nelly, from the LIV staff team, takes us out to dinner with a family. A mother with her two biological children and two adopted children. Ten of us in all sit down to eat and there is so much food we cannot begin to eat it all. Mama looked offended but we couldn't manage another mouthful. The food was strange to the boys but they did both try to eat the unfamiliar, as we have talked much about gratefully accepting hospitality. Even so, only James manages the cold banana custard for pudding. Conversation was stilted as there was no common language but we laughed, smiled, hugged and played with the children. We communicated what was important, love and gratitude, without words. The four of us were silent on the short walk home. All of us lost in our thoughts, observations and apprehensions of what the next five days would bring.

So I lie here, unable to sleep, wondering what on earth we can possibly give back to these people who have given already given us so much more than we expected.

## Friday 22nd February 2013

I don't need to worry about what we will do as we have a timetable. The boys, all three of them, are following one schedule. Girls, that's just me, another. I feel vulnerable and alone. Exposed, even. What if I can't do this? I have nowhere to run and no one to hide behind. It feels strange not to be with Josh and Toby. I know they are incredibly shy in new situations, and here there is nothing familiar. I can't help worrying that James won't notice when they are struggling, that he will get caught up in people and conversation and not notice when they need him. But for now I have to trust that they will be all right. I cannot be responsible for them. I need to do what is being asked of me. This morning I am helping with the babies, and the boys are going to school. We will meet at lunchtime for sports coaching. Swimming lessons and free play will fill our afternoon.

## Saturday 23rd February 2013

James is ill. He is rarely ill, or rather rarely makes a fuss about it, so I know he must be feeling terrible to have stayed in bed all day. There is a throat bug going around the village and it seems he has caught it. As much as he was the driving force behind us going on mission together, it is now just the three of us representing the family. I spent the morning in the school attending class violin lessons. It was great for me to see music being taught in a fresh, new way. I was inspired by the teaching methods and determined to take some ideas home with me. Only afterwards did I find out that, like the food in our fridge, like the houses that they are building, this was not just any violin teacher. This was the soloist with the Philharmonic Orchestra, about to appear on MTV later that day.

The boys have had to cope by themselves. They are still shy and finding everything strange. They are not sure of their roles. They are the same age as the children. Are they here to help, or attend school like one of the children? They don't know where they fit and I can't help them work it out. I don't know the answers for myself, let alone them. Why have we come on mission? Does five days of our time and presence make any difference to LIV village at all? Are we almost mission tourists?

There was one moment today when we knew ourselves to be useful. We were asked to spend our lunchtime helping in the stores. Each week the mothers are asked to put in a shopping list for the week. They just have to ask for what they need for their family. Supplies arrive, donated from local businesses, and the food is distributed. It is a huge task, fresh food for 100 people needing to be distributed quickly before it goes off in the ferocious heat. We enjoyed creating the boxes of shopping for each house, examining the strange ingredients. But there was so much more going on than simple shopping and food distribution. The mothers in the village are used to poverty, of having nothing. They find the system strange and have yet to learn to totally trust authority figures and white people, which goes against a lifetime of mistrust.

They have a duality in their minds of hoarding, anticipating a time when there will be nothing, therefore ordering way in excess of what their family could possibly need, and alternatively of failing to ask for what they need, as they can't quite trust in the provision. Each box, each delivery to a mother was a physical sign to them that they are loved, they are safe, they have value, they can trust. It will take more than food to change their hearts and minds, but to me it was just another way in which everything done in the village is to create a good life, a great life. Not just better than it was before, but the best that can be achieved. Through every action, every building, every conversation in LIV, people who had known situations I could not even begin to imagine, who had suffered more than I would ever know, were being shown love and value. Even their shopping mattered.

## Sunday 24th February 2013

James is still in bed. He is upset that he is missing out. It is our last day in LIV, and being Sunday we have no timetable, beyond an expectation that we will help at church. The people of the local town of Cottonlands are invited to worship alongside the village and the numbers of children attending Sunday school have soared in recent weeks. There are only a handful of staff to run church and Sunday school, and they knew that they would need our help. We were happy to be there. Fifty or so were expected, but in the end there were closer to seventy children in our group of five- to twelve-year-olds. Language was an issue, but communication was made more fun with an element of charades. There was much smiling and laughing and love, even if not much comprehension on my part! The first thing of Sunday school, before anything else, is to feed the children. Most children in Cottonlands will come to LIV without eating breakfast. They may not have lunch or dinner either that day. More important than anything else is feeding them, caring for them, showing them that they are loved. Besides, children can't learn anything if they are hungry, so the morning started with making what felt like hundreds of peanut-butter sandwiches, which literally disappeared before our eyes. From there we sang, we coloured, we listened to stories and we played games. It almost felt like a Sunday school that I could recognise, apart from the fact I did not understand a word that was said.

In the afternoon Josh, Toby and I went and just sat on the grass between the clusters of brightly coloured houses and talked and played with the children. We listened to the children's delight in their new home. Their new-found love for God. Their hopes and dreams for the future, which now for many, for the first time, seemed possible. One girl was hoping to be a photographer. Another, a lawyer. A few shared their heartbreaking stories with me. Guns, drugs, violence and rape were a common theme. But although my heart broke for them, they were not weeping. In our conversations that day they were not letting themselves be defined by their past, but rather saw themselves as set free by their present circumstances to pursue all their dreams. It was a precious few hours. James is missing out.

## Monday 25th February 2013

We only stayed in LIV for five days but they were unforgettable. We reluctantly leave to go on safari. The welcome in the village was so genuine, and the love displayed all around was undeniable. We helped in the crèche, the school, the church and the stores. We even coached sport. But perhaps most importantly of all we talked, we listened and we played. We received more than I ever imagined. I don't know what comes next. I have no answers as to why we went. But we were more than tourists. We got a glimpse of God's great goodness and love being poured out on earth. Like Mary after the birth of Jesus, I am storing up all the memories of our time at LIV and am treasuring them in my heart.[29] One day God will make sense of this. I am forever changed by our visit.

## Thursday 28th February 2013

Our five-star luxury glamping safari is not all we had hoped for. The safari is amazing. Rising before the dawn to drive out into the wilderness to catch a glimpse of the spectacular animals is all that I had anticipated. I have to confess a particular love of giraffe, and this morning when we could leave the jeep to walk with these giants was a moment I will never forget.

It's more that we have a problem with the glamping and the site where we are staying. It's not just the awkward transition from LIV to luxury, although that hasn't been easy. There are other niggles. For example, walking

---

[29] Luke 2:19.

between the tents, or when we are in the swimming pool, I find myself very aware of how flimsy the electric fence between me and the rhino appears. He is probably only 100 metres away and we have been told not to get too close. I keep wondering how close is too close. I'm not tempted to try to discover the answer. I'm not sure how fast a rhino can run, but I don't intend to find out. Then there are the monkeys that are all over the camp. James finds them cheeky and cute. I'm rather less enamoured. You have to watch yourself and your possessions at every turn. One stole a tea cup from our verandah and disappeared on to the roof to mime drinking tea. The next-door tent had their camera liberated. You can never leave a tent door open. They are everywhere, they are thieves and they are fearless.

The greatest problem of all, however, is inside the tent. At LIV in the stores we learned a very genuine fear of frogs, for we were taught that where there are frogs there are snakes. This knowledge has not been at all welcome when we find our tent full of frogs every evening as we return from dinner. In the shower, round the toilet, even in the beds. The first night we called to reception and asked them to remove the frogs. We were laughed at and humoured, but overnight the frogs returned en masse. By the morning the bathroom was a hopping, seething mass of frogs. Removing them was a pointless fight and we had to admit defeat. We keep a keen lookout for snakes.

## Monday 4th March 2013

It is always hard to get back into the swing of things after a holiday, but at the moment it is proving harder than I expected. We returned from the scorching heat of Johannesburg to snow at Heathrow. I had hoped that going away for the end of February would mean that we would be returning to daffodils and all the hopefulness of spring. Instead it is cold, slushy and dreary. It is hard not to want to be back in the warmth of Africa. However, James' confession as we drove to the airport of discovering a scorpion on the bathroom floor, and the memory of all those frogs, contrive to help me appreciate home a little bit more.

## Sunday 14th April 2013

Another Kit Kat, possibly my favourite yet. Jess organised a walk. It was simple and open to all. It was great to see her pride in organising something for everybody else. A small step for her in leadership. Throughout the walk I found myself alongside different people, chatting in a way that comes easily when you are engaged in something mutual. A welcome change to the intensity of organising to meet and talk over coffee. I love the way that these Sundays, which outwardly look nothing like church, do so much for the church. Relationships deepen and strengthen. People are discipled. All this stuff happens, almost unnoticed.

# Night Café

## Sunday 28th April 2013

For a long time James has wanted to start a night café. He is just unable to ignore the fact that Mary Arches Church is located opposite two nightclubs. This is where young people come and, if we are serious about going to meet them where they are, then this is where we need to be.

Last November James joined Street Pastors for possibly their wettest evening of the year. He returned absolutely shattered. Tired, yes. But more than that. He was shocked by what he had seen. The level of drunkenness, of violence. The broken bottles, the simmering violence, the language. Young people incapable and vulnerable after drinking too much. Abandoned by friends, either knowingly or unknowingly. Street Pastors have long been using our back room as a prayer base for their evenings spent in and around the town, but James saw the need for so much more.

So today church was opened up between 12 and 3am. Tea and toast were on offer. A place to be warm and safe.

Vomit kits and buckets were also freely available. To those standing in the queue to get into the nightclub, the church looked inviting. It had music and lights. We are not a club, but we don't look like a church either. They were intrigued, and they visited. They found a place of peace and calm. A place to wind down from the excesses outside. There were pool, table football, games consoles. It will take time to be known, to be accepted. We only have enough team to run one night café a month. We are not sure which night of the week is best. Friday or Saturday? Which night will be busiest? When can we connect with most people? To start with, depending on team availability, we will try both nights. In time we would love it to be a regular weekly refuge that could be relied upon, rather than on such an informal basis. We will need more team members.

## Sunday 9th June 2013

It is surprisingly hard to empty a baptistry. I'm not sure we considered the logistics of emptying what is essentially a full-sized paddling pool when we placed it in the north aisle of church. We'd thought about how to fill and heat it. We'd brought up our garden hose to run from the kitchen sink round into the church. It just reached. We had heaters in the water for most of Saturday and Sunday. It was still barely tepid when the baptism and confirmation service started. Emptying it proved way more of a challenge. We tried syphoning. However, the nearest window was five metres above the pool, and although the laws of physics were proved correct in our experiment – the water did drain – it was painfully slow. So we tried buckets. Much sloshing of water on the carpet, and many, many trips, but with a group effort and we managed it in the end.

The effort was all for Kyle and Josh who were baptised and confirmed by Bishop Nick this afternoon. We'd met both of these guys at Unlimited Goes Large, and have been journeying with them ever since. They are completely new to faith and have very little experience of church outside Unlimited. The service was laid-back and informal while being incredibly powerful. I think Josh, Kyle and others were pretty nervous about what it meant to have a bishop come to our church. The ice was well and truly broken when the bishop's mobile went off mid-service. James, of course, teased him. Everyone relaxed a fraction, they realised he is just a normal person, just like them.

## Saturday 29th June 2013

At 2am, a girl was brought into church who had lost her phone, keys, money and friends. Perhaps mercifully she was too drunk to appreciate the gravity of her situation. The team warmed her up and started trying to sort out what would happen for her next. She lived too far out for a taxi, and had no money to pay anyway. James walked in and uncharacteristically he recognised her. She lived in one of the villages where he had been team vicar. He managed to track down her address. Two of our team were driving back past her door, and at 4am delivered her safely home. We don't know if she appreciates how God protected her this morning, or what else could have happened. She may just think she was lucky. We know it is more than that and I am pleased we were there for her.

## Sunday 1st September 2013

First day of the new school. The boys have returned home taciturn, which is not unusual. From the little that I have gleaned most of Josh's conversations were about why he was at a girls' school. He is not amused. I hope he will be able to laugh about it one day. Not today. Today we will just eat pizza to celebrate new beginnings.

## Monday 2nd September 2013

I regret the passing of the holidays, but a new term does give me some space and time to think. I spent an hour in church today. The solitude was wonderful after the bustle and constant companionship of the summer. Mary Arches is such a wonderful Norman building. It has the potential to be a beautiful and welcoming space. But it isn't quite yet. It is chilly, shabby and a little bit messy (totally our fault – there is always something that we fail to put away). We still have no hot water. I think I would just repair the boiler while we pray about the bigger picture. But James doesn't agree. He is beginning to think we need to plan for more than toilets and a kitchen; we should make the space truly fit for purpose. With meeting rooms and offices. He is taking advice. It all sounds wonderful. And very far away.

## Tuesday 3rd September 2013

Pete and his wife, Rachel, have started coming to Unlimited. We have known them for such a long time and it is a delight that they have decided finally to join us. Chris and Sarah have also joined. It seems like we have been waiting for their wedding forever, and yet in truth we hardly know them. Both couples have only been with us for a fortnight and already there is a new energy within the team. They seem to be a part of all that we do. Every meeting and every event, they are there.

I worry for Chris and Sarah. They are newly married and new to Exeter and have committed to arranging their diary and social lives around church, putting church first. I am concerned for their busyness. When we got married, our church made us stop all church activities, groups, serving and outreach for six months. Actually, the church usually advised married couples to treasure the whole of the first year of marriage in this way. The idea was to give time and space to a couple to form a strong, new family unit from which to reach out. We could only manage six months to fit in with James' training requirements.

I loved those first six months. I treasured evenings together and time with James. He does not have the same fond memories. I remember his sheer delight when the six months were up and he could get back to doing what he loved. It would have been easy to be offended, to have taken it personally, but the truth is he just loves people, loves God and is passionate about connecting the two. I remember this time now as I would love to protect Chris and Sarah in the early days of their marriage. To not overwhelm them with church meetings, outreach events, prayer. But the truth is, we need them. We simply don't have enough people in church. They are keen to get stuck straight in and, with only slight misgivings, we let them.

Pete and Rachel, Chris and Sarah, James and Ruth: three newly married couples, all in their twenties. What a wonderful start to married life. To be embedded in a church seeking after the heart of God with friends that can both support and encourage you. I love them all, am starting to be friends with them all. But already I can see that their friendship bonds will go deeper. Their shared stage of life will bind them together in a way that I can't join in. I can't help being a little bit jealous.

# Units

*Thursday 10th October 2013*

Organisation is not our strong point. Historically we have been good at muddling along. We've had to be adaptable and spontaneous. Everyone pitching in with all aspects of church life. Setting up chairs, clearing away, washing-up, welcome, whatever. Now that there are more people in Unlimited, it's no longer working. The same small group of people seem to do everything, and all the while they grow ever more aware and resentful of those who are sitting around chatting. I am also being talked to more and more by people who feel they don't fit in, that the church has cliques, that they feel excluded from friendships. So we have divided the church into Units. On the outside they look as though they are about the practical set-up and hospitality in church. Our hope is that they will be so much more than that. Small groups where people are known and loved, where they are valued and can build friendships and have fun.

## Thursday 7th November 2013

More sex. Again James and I went in as a couple to answer questions on our marriage. We are becoming old hands at it now. We have learned to actively encourage all the questions we had thought we would want to avoid. The quicker they get them out of the way, the quicker the ice is broken, the quicker we can start to share with them something much more important than the details of our sex life.

I'm much more comfortable with the young people but I was still awkward at the school gate when I was innocuously asked, 'What have you been doing today?' I fumbled the answer and wasn't entirely truthful. I still find it hard to talk about sex.

## Sunday 24th November 2013

Laura got baptised today. She is a bright, bubbly drama student. She seems to be always laughing and smiling. Over the past year she has gradually got to know us and trust us. God has steadily been drawing her back to this point, drawing her back into a living relationship she knew as a child. Today she publicly acknowledged her faith before friends and family. It was a big deal for her. She wanted to share her testimony, but not all the details. She felt the need to be honest without revealing everything. I knew how nervous she was, but I doubt few others realised. The drama student in her won through, and she spoke clearly and confidently. She let us in on her journey with a trust and vulnerability that was amazing. She made us laugh with her. She trusted us with her struggles.

She told us that when she was younger she had gone to church every Sunday, and loved it. She had loved learning about all the amazing things that Jesus did for everyone, she loved learning that there was a God out there watching over us. At that time church was a place where she felt safe. Then, before Laura turned twelve, everything changed. A series of events led to her father leaving her family, and from that point on, in her words 'everything was wrong'. Her family fell apart, her life was torn to pieces, she stopped being able to trust. Her faith disintegrated as she couldn't understand why it had all happened – why God had allowed it. In her pain and confusion, she stopped going to church. She was hurting and there was nowhere safe any more. Through her teenage years she managed to hold her life together, although it took all her strength and determination not to fall apart. She thought that she needed to be strong for everyone. She didn't trust in anything or anyone but herself.

In January of this year she met two of our team, Ben and Alison, on the Cathedral Green. Apparently their first conversation was not a huge success. Laura was not at all keen to talk to them. During the conversation they did manage to invite her to Unlimited, but she really didn't want to go with them. However, after they left she was intrigued, and in the end she came to visit us just to see what we were like. She told us, 'I've never met such a wonderful group of people!' From that first contact she started to come along more often. She loved our joy, and our love and excitement. But nothing changed in her life, she was still relying on herself, her own strength. It took a bit of a drunken breakdown for her to realise that she wasn't living her life how she should have been, and at that point she accepted Jesus back into her life again.

Her life didn't change radically overnight. Every day continues to be a struggle. But what has changed completely is that she now knows that she's never alone. That she doesn't need to rely only on herself to do things. She is learning to trust again. She has found that love and joy she had as a child when she went to church. She has rediscovered her fascination with the Bible and how it speaks to us. But most importantly of all, she feels safe again. Safe with God – knowing that He is with her always.

I will never forget her bravery in sharing, trusting us with her story. I will also never forget the location. Baptism in the church building was something we have struggled with. Using a font with adults bending over doesn't seem to fully convey the symbolism of dying and raising to new life in Christ. Previously we had borrowed a baptistry. Both filling and emptying were not trivial. We considered, briefly, going to the seaside. We discarded it quickly as being way too chilly in winter. So in a moment of brilliance, or madness, I suggested that we should indeed be unlimited by culture and tradition and we should hire a local swimming pool. Many local pools were available for birthday party hire on a Sunday afternoon, so that is what we did. After the formal service, and the very strange acoustic in which we worshipped, the pool was transformed by a giant inflatable obstacle course. The whole church (almost) jumped in, and the party and the fun continued. It was an unforgettable, unusual day of celebration.

# Live Lounge

*Saturday 30th November 2013*

Tonight saw possibly 100 young people in the church. Music seems to be such a part of young people's lives. So many that we meet are either in a band or are friends with someone in a band. Tonight we simply opened up church and offered them a microphone. Cheekily we called it Live Lounge after the Radio 1 show. And the bands came and brought their supporters. Some of the music was amazing. Not all was to my taste, but then it shouldn't be. If it is appealing to me as a nearly forty-year-old then I'm guessing we've got it wrong. But it was about more than music. Every bit of available space in church was put to use to show the young people that they matter, that making them feel comfortable and welcome in our space was important to us. We had drinks, a nail bar that they thought was for pampering but was actually an excuse to be able to engage in conversation, games consoles projected on to the ceiling, giant garden games.

I spent most of the evening in the back room preparing hundreds of hot dogs. I can't deny that the smell was appalling. Halfway through the evening food was shared around, and there was a brief moment where James told them why we were doing all of this. That actually, unashamedly, this was all about Jesus. Of course, some left and others switched off. But more, I think, were intrigued. Several asked for prayer from the team, and the team then had the very great privilege of helping these young people encounter God. Some young people learned, perhaps for the first time, that God is not distant and apart, looking down from his seat on a fluffy white cloud. He is right here with them now. And He knows them and He loves them.

For the young people affected by tonight, they still have a journey ahead of them. We are grateful to be able to journey with them.

## Sunday 1st December 2013

I'm on my knees tonight. I've been getting it so wrong and it took my eleven-year-old son to expose me. I've taken myself away from the family, from time together, to say sorry for what I've become. I need time to come before God to say I'm sorry. True repentance, walking in the opposite spirit, will take time. But it's a journey I'm beginning tonight. I'm starting with a heartfelt plea for forgiveness for where I've been getting it so wrong.

The problem is that I've been talking about people. Not to them, about them. Often as we drive home from church, James will ask us all the question, 'What did you think of tonight?' I had started to use that invitation to share my thoughts about people, and to my shame as I reflect on what Josh said, my words haven't always been positive. In fairness, my thoughts about people haven't been all negative. I just guess that I haven't voiced many positive ones in front of the boys. Instead what they've been hearing is where I've allowed my petty frustrations to linger. I've not been keeping short accounts with people. I've actually been keeping a record of everyone's wrongs and I've been using the journey home to air them all. I've become centred on me. I've become selfish and self-absorbed. Poor me that we always have to turn up early for set-up. Poor me that we are always last to leave after clearing away. I've noticed and resented people when they are late, when they aren't where they said they'd be, when they don't do what they said they'd do. In truth I'd stopped seeing the people that I love, and had started to see them in terms of what they did and didn't do. I was finding that the problem with a small church was that there were always jobs that needed doing and never enough people to do them. I'd started seeing church members, my friends, in terms of what they could do rather than who they were. I'd stopped just loving them because they were friends and instead started measuring them constantly in how they were performing. Attendance. Service. Doing. I'd forgotten how to just 'be' and I'd stopped letting others just 'be' too.

Over many journeys home from church that is all my family have heard from me. But tonight it stops. I want to speak life over people, when they are with me or when they are not. I don't want to ever say stuff behind someone's back that I wouldn't say to their face. I don't want my children to find me a hypocrite. I'm not going to teach one thing and live something totally different.

Tomorrow I start walking out my repentance. Pouring out blessing on people, whether I think they deserve it or not, Because what I think they deserve just doesn't come into it. God loves them. He wants to bless them. And I want to be a part of that.

## Wednesday 15th January 2014

It feels right that now is the time to think about expanding our staff team. With just James, myself, an intern and a handful of volunteers, we all feel stretched too thinly. We were amazed when out of the blue Pete approached us to ask if we would consider him being our youth worker while he studies for a degree in applied theology at Moorlands College. He is considering giving up his well-paid job as a graphic designer in Bristol to come and work with us. He would be placed with us as a youth worker while studying part-time. He would bring an amazing set of skills, beyond his obvious love for young people, but it is a placement and we would have to pay to support him. We have no money. We think it is the right thing for us and the right thing for Pete, but he needs to make a decision and commit to his course before we can absolutely guarantee the money. It is easy for me to encourage him to step out in faith as it is not me putting everything on the line.

## Sunday 2nd March 2014

After a year of prayer we are nearly there. Thirty-seven members! I can manufacture explanations as to why we are not forty. There are those who slipped away during the year, who turned their back on faith. But I don't need to explain it away. It is an answer to prayer. Our church feels doubled in size. On a Sunday we are often way more than forty. Thirty-seven is the number who have filled in the official form, are baptised, have committed to giving and actively serve the mission. Many more come to us just to be with us, to be at church. Not ready to commit, but aware that this is something they want to be a part of.

God calls us to be unlimited in our expectations of Him. He can do more than we can possibly hope for or imagine.[30] This is just the first step. I wonder what will follow.

---

[30] See Ephesians 3:20.

# Awkward

*Monday 10th March 2014*

I went out for coffee today. Nothing unusual in me doing that on a Monday. I often pop for a coffee between harp pupils as a way to stretch my legs and clear my head. But I was taken aback by the welcome I received. Usually the couple who run the shop are effusive and chatty. We share something of our days, our weeks. Not today. They didn't want to talk at all. I was worried I had offended them somehow. I left confused and saddened.

I told James my worries this evening. He could see I was carrying something, chewing it over and over. Although it seemed trivial, unimportant, it still mattered to me. I couldn't shake it off. When I told him what was wrong he started laughing. I wasn't amused. I felt he wasn't taking me seriously. But he then explained that for the last six weeks he has also been going to that coffee shop with Ruth early on a Monday morning. Ruth has stayed in Exeter since finishing her degree. She has always been passionate about working with young girls. She is brilliant at listening to them, encouraging them, being there for them. They find it easy to relate to her. At twenty-five she is neither the age to be their mother nor their friend, and I have rarely seen girls respond to her other than with respect and love. She is someone they can turn to, can trust and can confide in. It is Ruth's joy that she can spend so much time doing what she is passionate about alongside studying for her master's degree in sports psychology. Since January James and Ruth have been running a Romance Academy course in St Luke's school, a place where young people can look at issues of identity and self-worth in a safe environment. There is an awkward time gap for James and Ruth between dropping the boys at school and the start of the Romance Academy session, and so rather than wasting it they have taken to planning the sessions in this coffee shop. I began to totally understand the coffee shop owners' response earlier in the day.

This morning my husband was in this very small, friendly shop, where many conversations are communal, with a stunningly beautiful young lady. And they were talking through the course. This morning's topics were pregnancy, sexually transmitted diseases and contraception.

I'm not surprised the owners didn't know what to say to me. I wouldn't have, either. Somehow I will have to let them know that I know, and that it's OK.

# Dreaming Dreams

*Friday 14th March 2014*

God has expanded our vision. Rather than an extra toilet and a few kitchen cupboards, we are now thinking of so much more. What if Mary Arches could become a youth hub for the city centre, the place for young people to come when they need some help? A centre with pregnancy crisis counselling, drop-in … Anything that is needed. We now have a vision to transform the church. To build a proper kitchen, to install meeting rooms, quiet spaces, offices. And, of course, toilets. We are looking at a quarter of a million pounds worth of change, probably. And amazingly we have been promised the money. After James had preached at a local church, a man came up to him and asked if he could help our vision in any way. He runs a trust fund from money that his late wife apparently won on the lottery. They have met, together they dreamed dreams and now an exciting plan is coming together. We have contacted an architect, and started the formal process with the diocese.

## Tuesday 20th May 2014

Pete and Rachel have made their decision. They are in! Incredibly, the money also seems certain. The trust fund should cover all Pete's expenses, and if not, then James has a personal guarantee that Pete will be paid. I am so relieved, I can't imagine how Pete and Rachel are feeling.

## Saturday 31st May 2014

I am still surprised when people assume that I know what they talked to James about when they met him last week. There is a joke in the church that James and I never talk to each other. I smile when it is said, but it doesn't make me laugh. It comes from an assumption that we share every detail of every conversation. We don't. We can't. Some days we are thankful to have five quiet minutes together. Many more days we have none. Yes, we have time together, but often with the boys around. Also we are busy, and we work hard to make sure that church is not the only thing we talk about, the only thing we have in common. I never know whether to pretend I do know (Do they want me to know? Does it feel like I don't care? Did they want it to be confidential?), or tell them that we have other things in our life, and it's James' job, not mine. Generally I smile and shrug and play it by ear. Hopefully I get it right most of the time.

## Thursday 10th July 2014

There's no money. Nothing. The quarter of a million isn't coming. Apparently the board of the trust fund will not agree to it. The building project is on hold. Not abandoned, but definitely on hold. But worse than that, much worse, there is no money for Pete and Rachel. They have given up everything, their jobs and their flat and we have nothing to offer. It had seemed too good to be true. Too easy. And it was. It is as though the promise of the money helped us to dream big, and we did! We expanded our vision and now have an idea of something incredible, something which I still think God wants us to pursue. Only now it will be so much harder. As I never met the man, this all feels like a slight fantastical interlude, but James is struggling so much more. He met him. He trusted him. He liked him. He feels so let down. He is working through the feelings, but it is a work in progress. He can see that this enabled us to dream big, but at the moment James cannot be grateful for that. He feels angry and responsible for letting Pete down. Yet despite his inner turmoil and all the uncertainty we now face over the way forward, James still has a sense of peace. Maybe God has another plan.

## Sunday 14th September 2014

Pete has started work for us. We have three months' pay in the bank, but that is all. Our only hope for finance beyond that rests with two trust applications that we have made. If the applications aren't successful, then we will have to let him go. It doesn't bear thinking about. But for now we have a staff team of four. A weekly staff meeting has been instigated. His focus is on outreach and mission to youth, leaving James more free to run the church, to pastor the members. We hope Pete will push us outside our comfort zone and not let us stand still or get complacent. We want him to feel free to start new initiatives, to link up with youth in ways we haven't thought of yet. I am impatient to see him do all of this.

## Tuesday 14th October 2014

11pm. James has just told me that he has an assembly in the morning and that he doesn't know what he is going to say. This alone would be enough to keep me wide awake. I would have paper, pens, internet, books all arrayed in a frenzy of planning. He has just gone to sleep. In his role as chaplain to the local secondary school he has to give many assemblies, as well as being in demand in five other schools. I would be in a panic if I were him. We are so different. I have long since learned that him telling me he hasn't prepared a talk yet does not mean that he wants my input. It is literally just for my information. Whenever I have tried to help him, the conclusion from all my great ideas is often that he now knows what he doesn't want to say. So I have given up trying to help him, as often my efforts are actually just trying to make him more like me. If I were giving an assembly it would be planned a week in advance, and have been practised multiple times. His preparation does not look like mine. He continually thinks, absorbs and mulls and then comes out with brilliant, engaging talks. He writes notes, but it is a standing joke that his notes bear very little relation to what he actually says.

## Wednesday 5th November 2014

After a weekend of being in a darkened room, the curtains have been opened on to a dazzling new world. After years of indecision, I finally had laser surgery on my eyes on Friday. Apart from the issue of vanity, although I do hate wearing glasses, I had been persuaded it was the best and healthiest option for my eyes as contact lenses were causing me so many troubles. The pain of the weekend was indescribable. But almost as suddenly as it started, it finished. As promised, almost to within the minute, forty-eight hours after the procedure I found I was no longer counting the minutes until the next pain relief could be administered. I know the worst is behind me. I must be in a better place because James has finally left me home alone. He has gone to meet Jo. She is on holiday in Devon and has asked to meet James for a coffee. We work with her every year at Soul Survivor festivals. She has always seemed very nice, but we know very little about her. James has no idea why she wants to meet.

# Trusting God

## Thursday 6th November 2014

It's one thing to believe in what you are called to do. To follow God faithfully, even when what you are called to do feels too much for you. But when others catch your vision and want to join in, that is an indescribable encouragement. Any thought of feeling weary or sorry for yourself is banished as they bring fresh hope, encouragement and energy. And that is what happened yesterday. Jo wanted to meet James to talk about joining Unlimited. It seems she is prepared to sell her house, leave her job and move to Exeter because she thinks God is calling her here. That she has been in Nottingham for more than eighteen years, was at university there and has never left means she has built a life rich with friends, connections and love that will be incredibly painful to leave. She knows she will have to sacrifice much. And yet she still wants to come. I'm so excited. She brings age, wisdom and maturity to the church.

On a much more personal note, she is my age. Finally I would have a peer within the church. A friend, maybe.

## Thursday 4th December 2014

Four hours of teaching in a classroom has confirmed what I always suspected – I would be a terrible secondary school teacher. Throughout my life people have variously told me I ought to teach physics. They have told me that there is a shortage of women in science and they appear to think that I personally should do something about it. I have always resisted. I love teaching, but I love teaching students who want to learn. Who have opted in. So I teach music, tutor at home, have taught maths and physics in universities. My worry is that physics is a fairly unpopular subject at school, so you are already facing an uphill battle before you even start. I fear that I would be neither engaging nor inspiring enough to capture the imagination of the students, and so the lessons would descend into being much more about crowd control than the subject intended.

Perhaps today was not a totally fair test of my abilities as a secondary school teacher. As a team we had not set ourselves the easiest of tasks. Two two-hour sessions with over-excited Year Nines talking about sex. We have been invited to partner with the local school in their Personal, Social and Health Education (PSHE) provision, and it is a great opportunity. A vote of confidence in us as a church and all that we do. It just wasn't easy. So much of school sex education seems to cover the act itself. There was much talk of cucumbers and condoms from the pupils through the morning. But we wanted to take a different approach. We attempted to get them to discover more about themselves, their choices and their capacity for building lasting relationships. We wanted them to understand the importance of emotions in this whole area. We had games, quizzes, group discussions, talks, videos. I was paired with Pete and the session was fast-paced, engaging and utterly exhausting. Unavoidably there was a lot of giggling and ribald comments before we started. Everyone felt uncomfortable: Pete, me and the pupils. But we set some ground rules, some boundaries of how we would honour and respect one another in the process.

In the end I think it went well. It was certainly exhausting. Trying constantly to get them to engage on topic was a challenge. It was interesting that it seemed that these young guys and girls appear to fall into two quite distinct groups at this age. Those who think they know absolutely all there is to know about sex, and those for whom it hasn't even entered their thinking yet. Holding both groups and moving them forward together was a sensitive task.

We will know what to expect next time. I will get better at this.

## Wednesday 7th January 2015

We are continuing with the building project; of course we are. It will just be so much slower. We are still sure it is the right thing, it is just less urgent now, and definitely more daunting. We will have to find the quarter of a million from somewhere. But that is not the immediate problem. We can't reorder the building until we have a long-term rental agreement in place. As a BMO we rent the church from the parish on a yearly agreement. We will need a much longer agreement in place before we can start to change anything about the building. Honestly, I'm not totally sure why we have to pay rent. I've had it explained to me several times, but in the end as it is all God's kingdom and all the Church of England it does feel a little like money-shuffling to me.

Anyway, it's in hand, it's with the solicitors, but it does feel as though everything has ground to a halt. In my limited experience, the lawyers seem to be moving very slowly.

## Wednesday 8th April 2015

It is so easy to get it wrong with money. To hold on too tight and to let it become a master over you, to let fear control your thinking, your spending and your generosity. Or to go to the other extreme and trust God for everything without taking any personal responsibility. From my family I picked up a view that saving is 'good', spending is 'bad'. I was never taught this, but certainly by the time I went to university this was my informed opinion. I regarded my grant as savings and did everything I could to avoid spending it. I was terrified of running out of money. I didn't really know this was so ingrained in me. While James and I were dating, he paid for pretty much everything as I always felt I couldn't afford to do stuff. It all came out when we got married and we opened our first joint bank account. In that account we shared 'all that we had' and we were both shocked to discover that I had saved £2,000 during my student years, mostly at his expense. That realisation began in me a process of trusting God with my money. Of actively walking in the opposite spirit. Of being generous, even when it felt unnatural, or sometimes even wrong. I think for me I will always struggle in this area, but I am determined to keep on growing and trusting. So I'm encouraged and surprised to find it so much easier to trust God for all that we need as church than I do for me personally. As bad as being let down over promised funding was for James, somehow I knew God had it all in hand. Being one step removed from the nitty-gritty of the application process for grants probably helped me trust in the big picture. But I was not surprised to hear this morning that all the money has come through to fund Pete for four years. Two charities are each giving us substantially more than they normally award in grants. The relief in James is palpable. I am delighted for Pete and Rachel.

# Unravelled

## Sunday 10th May 2015

It is time to try something new. Attendance at Kit Kat has been going down and down. Rather than us gathering as church just for the sake of being together, of spending time with one another, it has become widely regarded as a Sunday off. It has become an unhelpful part of the tradition of our church, so it is time to change.

Instead, on a monthly basis we are going to gather as church to grapple with controversial topics. It will be a space where everyone is totally welcome to come, whatever their opinions, and it will be a space where every opinion can be safely expressed. My idea was that we would gather around afternoon tea. I offered to provide the first one, to set the bar, so I have spent the morning getting it ready. I can't go this afternoon, or rather we decided I shouldn't go. The first topic we're looking at is *Fifty Shades of Grey*. A book that so many people are reading and talking about at the moment but something the boys are oblivious to, and I'm happy to keep it that way. It doesn't happen often, but every now and then there are things that we want and need to discuss in church that the boys really don't need to know about yet. Even with our protection, I'm aware that they understand more about such subjects as relationships, depression and eating disorders than many boys their age. But if I can't attend then my contribution is the tea – cheese and ham, ham and cucumber, cheddar and chutney, salmon and cream cheese sandwiches; freshly baked scones; and double chocolate chip muffins. It is a feast I'm proud of. It feels strange to be sitting at home wondering how it is going. I look forward to joining in next month.

## Tuesday 12th May 2015

Another crazy idea from James? Or God-inspired? I'm not sure. I have to trust his vision. His enthusiasm is infectious. He wants to persuade the cathedral to hold an outreach event for thousands of young people. A bigger, better version of the party we put on at the cathedral in 2009 to celebrate 1,100 years of the diocese. With all the local churches joining together for the young people of Exeter. The obvious date looks like being on the Queen's ninetieth birthday next year, so we could sell it as a huge birthday party. He's imagining a skate park, a football cage, a pamper zone, giant inflatables, as well as big screen gaming, live bands, a talk and more. It sounds great. It sounds like a lot of work. He will need a strong team around him.

# God Encounters

## Sunday 5th July 2015

I haven't been to an ordination since James was ordained in Christ Church, Oxford, seventeen years ago. This weekend I have been delighted to go to two.

On Saturday we went to the splendid setting of St Paul's Cathedral to see Ed get ordained. We were so grateful to be able to celebrate this special day with both Ed and Jess, who is now his wife. It was the amazing culmination of a journey that started with Unlimited. Since leaving us he has worked for two other churches, one in Sunningdale and the other Holy Trinity Brompton. We haven't managed to keep in touch as we would like, but he shared with us during the day that the time he spent at Unlimited had a big impact on his decision to offer himself forward for ordained ministry. He loved the opportunities to reach out to the next generation and realised with us that God was calling him to give his life to be a part of leading His church. It is so encouraging to hear this, but we are so aware that whatever he learned from us, he gave us as a church and as a family so much more than we gave to him. Both Ed and Jess were such an important part of the Unlimited journey we are excited to see what God has in store for them in the years to come.

Then on Sunday we turned to modern from ancient. Not the lofty grandeur of St Paul's, but the stark modernity of Guildford Cathedral. I rather liked the contrast. Today we went to support Eileen. She has been our friend for eight years. It was an unlikely friendship as she joined the staff team at St John's Harborne only a few weeks before we left. But life, circumstances and God had other ideas and over the years we have got to know her very well. She has become an incredibly dear friend. She is an inspiration to me. She has stuck with God through some awful times, when it would have been easier to turn away. She refuses to be defined by what has been, and even though at times it has been a painful and frustratingly slow process she has doggedly carried on, determined not to get stuck in a moment. I am surprised that she stayed friends with us. Sometimes those who have seen you at your lowest are those you would rather forget when life improves. Not so with Eileen. After years of her visiting and us listening, praying, supporting, encouraging (or in her words, 'poking'!) her to keep going, she keeps coming back to visit. The visits are now joyful and full of laughter. And they should be; she and God have turned her life around. Today we celebrate her ordination. Next year we will dance at her wedding. Not something that she ever thought would happen. Not something that any of us take for granted. There is so much to be thankful for this weekend.

Two amazing people, our friends, starting a lifetime of offering themselves to God within the Church of England.

## Sunday 16th August 2015

I've spent so much time worrying that I'm not good enough, that I can't do what God is asking of me. But today God showed me again that I've been getting it all wrong. It was through a seminar at Soul Survivor. When God, through the burning bush,[31] called Moses to return to Egypt and ask Pharaoh to set His people free, Moses felt weak and pointed out to God all the reasons why he was the wrong person for the job. Honestly, at that point I was only half-listening. James was the seminar speaker and his words were very familiar. I thought I knew the story backward and I had nothing new to learn. I was busy thinking through all the reasons why Moses was exactly the right person. All the things that I would tell him if I were God. The fact that he was raised in Pharaoh's Palace while knowing his heritage as a Hebrew uniquely placed him with both sides. His passion for justice had been expressed, albeit wrongly, when he killed an Egyptian for unfair treatment of a slave. But in that moment God did not point any of this out to him. He didn't show him his CV. He did not speak to him about how Moses had been prepared for exactly this purpose. He didn't even go on to say, 'It's not about you, it's about Me.' No, God simply said to Moses: 'I'll be with you.' The important thing, the only thing for Moses, is who goes with him.

---

[31] Exodus 3-4.

It's not about me. It's about who is with me. A simple thought. So if it's not about me, but about who is with me, then I will step up into all that God is calling me. I will spend less time thinking about why I'm not good enough, and more time knowing that God is enough.

## Tuesday 18th August 2015

One of our young people, Chris, has just become a Christian! He came with us to Soul Survivor and had very few expectations of the event. We first met him earlier this year at a Wednesday café. Weeks later the team got to pray for him and he couldn't believe what he was hearing. In his words, their prayers were 'bang on'! He was completely thrown. He kept returning to church. He liked us. He said we had a 'great vibe'. We were surprised and pleased when he agreed to come with us to Soul Survivor. It is not always easy to persuade young people to come to a Christian event in a field in Somerset. But he came, and it was brilliant seeing his face as he entered the Big Top – he said he had no idea there were that many Christians in the UK, let alone in one tent! Today he was being prayed for, and when the team started praying about anger he apparently started to feel really weird. Weirder than when he had been prayed for before, and that was the moment he decided that he wanted to jump straight in and become a Christian. Such great news.

He's part of our family now.

# Life Continues

## Thursday 10th September 2015

Units have not worked. The groups became all about the practicalities of serving and lost any sense of pastoral care for the members. Commitment to actually turning up when your Unit was on the rota was low, and so the few Unit members who did turn up felt under increasing amounts of pressure. Tensions between those that got on with the job and those who actively avoided it were possibly worse within a small group than when it was in the larger setting. Sadly, we have to disband. We remain convinced, however, that smaller groups, places where we are known, are the key to belonging. And the jobs remain. As we grow, there are ever more things to do. More chairs and beanbags to place out, more tea and coffee to serve, more cake to bake, more washing-up. So we have rebranded! TEDs started this month. Named TEDs[32] as they are a little part of Unlimited. (We offered the name as

---

[32] Not related to TED talks.

a joke to the leadership, and were amazed when they didn't laugh!) Again a small group, but this time first and foremost is the relationship. Each month we will take a Tuesday out and, instead of eating together as a whole church in Mary Arches, TEDs will meet in homes. A group of people gathering together for an evening of food and fun. Each TED will look different. After eating, some will pray. Some will study the Bible. Some will play games. It doesn't matter what each group looks like, what matters is that they get together. That they get to know each other. That they belong.

## Sunday 18th October 2015

James and Ruth are leaving today. Job promotions and degrees are taking them away from Exeter. Our whole family will miss them. In church we will be poorer without their friendship and their vitality, the way that they connect so easily with everyone and draw people together. But perhaps for the first time I am not fearful of someone leaving. They will create holes, of course they will. No one else will be able to fill the gaps that they leave. They were part of the team that started the company, that prayed through every aspect of what Unlimited should be while it remained merely a hope for the future. They are part of our creation story. James has been the only treasurer the company has ever known. As well as being a director, Ruth has come alongside many vulnerable young girls. She has been our safeguarding officer. But as I think about them leaving Unlimited, I am secure in the knowledge that we have, and always will have, exactly the people we need for what we are called to do. God will bring us more people and resources in His timing. It is not my place to worry. I'm free from fear. I'm learning to trust.

So we party to say goodbye in Unlimited style. I'm sad to lose my friends, but I'm not afraid of what lies ahead.

## Friday 6th November 2015

People never seem to get bored of the age-old witticism, 'Of course, you only work on Sundays, don't you?' We hear that on a more or less weekly basis. I presume they are joking. I've got to think that or else it would really start to wind me up. But even if they have given any thought to what James' work might be beyond the obvious on a Sunday, I'm guessing they would be totally wrong about today.

He, and about ten team members from church, have spent the day on Dartmoor. Climbing, abseiling and doing high ropes in the middle of a forest. In torrential rain. A team-building activity day. It was wet, cold and great fun, I'm told. With them were ten students from St Luke's school, students who had been identified by the school as struggling or vulnerable in some way, and this is the start of a mentoring programme. Over the next school year, our team will meet one-on-one with these guys. Once a fortnight for a coffee, or more likely a can of drink, and to give them a space to be listened to. To be able to talk and to be valued. We don't know what will happen. Whether it will work. Whether they will want to talk. Today they just got to break the ice and to get to know each other. James returned from an unusual day at the office very muddy.

## Saturday 7th November 2015

I have been finding the toll that Night Café takes on the whole family too much, and I have questioned whether it is the right thing to continue. Although I am not the one that goes, it eats into our time together. James' day off is a Saturday. I know many clergy take a weekday off, but I've never liked the idea of him being off one day in the week when the children are at school, and then him working when they are around. We tried it, but it wasn't right for us, so we returned to Saturday being his day off. It isn't ideal. It means he works hard Monday to Friday, has Saturday off and then is straight back to work on Sunday. The idea that I've heard some vicars suggest of only doing work that comes to them on a Saturday, leading to a lighter day, is not our experience. So, on our precious day off when James would happily sleep until 11am or later, and we are creeping around trying not to disturb him, it is hard not to resent the fact that I think this is family time.

But today he shared a story from last night, and perhaps I am wrong. Maybe it is where he should be, and we pay a very small price for that. Apparently last night a couple of lads came in. One of them regularly attends Wednesday café, the other one had been a couple of times. As James got chatting with him, the guy James barely knows told of how a few weeks ago he'd been really low, on the verge of suicide. He said as he was lying on his bed thinking about how to end his life, he saw the cards which the team had written on when they prayed for him. They had prayed, as we have done for hundreds of others, about how God saw him, what it was in him that was unique and special. As a team we always write down these prayers so that the young people can keep them and think about them. We encourage them to reject them where the team have got it wrong, but we also hope it will help them to remember a point where God spoke into their lives. This guy told how when he reread what had been written, he changed his mind. He no longer wanted to end his life.

## Thursday 12th November 2015

The cathedral has said 'yes' to the huge party/outreach on the Queen's ninetieth birthday. We have a name for the event. It will be called Upload. Mike Pilavachi is coming to speak. Bands are booked. This may all fall into place.

## Friday 27th November 2015

It's good to be able to laugh at ourselves. As a church we take God very seriously, ourselves not so much! Because of that atmosphere, that it's all right to give it a go, everything doesn't have to be perfect. Tonight I did give it a go. I put aside what other people might think, whether I was good enough. I just gave it a go, with the knowledge that if I did my best, then no matter what happened, that was all God asked of me. Oh, and not to give myself a hard time if it didn't live up to my own standards of perfection. So I took a slot at Live Lounge. We knew that this time there weren't as many bands coming as usual, so Pete had encouraged anyone who could to prepare a song so that we could fill the gaps when the mic was empty. I've never wanted to before, but today it felt that it could be fun. So I spent the afternoon messing around with electric harp and voice, working out my arrangement of a pop song, and tonight I performed. It wasn't perfect. I'm glad it wasn't recorded. But I did my best. I had fun. That was all God wanted from me tonight.

## Friday 26th February 2016

In my determination not to resent Night Café I've tried to turn the time we're waiting for James to wake into something special rather than let it feel like wasted space. Josh, Toby and I are doing a tour of local cafés and pubs in a quest to find the best breakfast in Exeter. As treats go, it is not too expensive, they love breakfast, and it makes it a day we look forward to, rather than dread. Today we returned home to find James awake and waiting for us. The boys are always relieved to see him up and in one piece. They find it hard to forget the time he returned home after being punched.

They are always keen to hear his stories about Night Café, though, as long as no one gets hurt. In many ways, to those of us who have slept innocently through the night, his stories can seem as though from a foreign land. We are always intrigued. James didn't disappoint. Last night was a tale of three girls. Before café started, during prayer, one of the team had been reminded of the moment in the film *The Hunchback of Notre Dame* when Quasimodo comes in declaring about sanctuary. Much later a small group came into the café. Two of the group were quite drunk and very distressed with each other. The third, the sister of one of them, was reasonably sober and trying to keep the peace. Apparently one girl had got into trouble on the dance floor and, as a result, the other one had been set upon. She was scared and very angry. The team removed the two drunk girls from each other and cared for them separately. The sister kept going back and forth between them. After a while, she said, 'This place reminds me of the *Hunchback of Notre Dame* and sanctuary!'

God knew that they were coming to café today. We were where He wanted us to be.

## Thursday 3rd March 2016

I've never done this before. I went into an estate agent at midday and picked up the keys for a new house. Not my new house. This is for Jo. After sixteen months of planning, job applications, house buying and selling, finally today she has her home. It has been such a difficult and uncertain process that she was unable to make the start of her new job coincide with the timings of the house sale. For the next six weeks she will own a house in Exeter but continue working in Nottingham, and will be forced to live on the kindness and generosity of friends who will provide her with a temporary base. She will have to do a lot of driving. In fact, the sale was so uncertain right up until the last minute she was unable even to book any annual leave, and so it is that we are taking possession of the house for her. We go round with the intention of cleaning but find the house is spotless. She will arrive later tonight, if the M5 is kind. I hope it marks the start of a new beginning for her as she has needed great determination to get to this point. Often it would have been easier and totally understandable if she had decided to change her mind, and not relocate. But through these months I have learned that she is fierce and tough, and she has doggedly continued through every setback and challenge placed before her. She has visited Exeter several times. Driven hundreds of miles. Joined in countless church events she was unwilling to miss. And over these many visits we have become friends. We have a shared love of running, of cooking, of caring for people. Her new house is a few minutes' walk away from me. We are now neighbours. We both hope this will work out.

# Rhythm of Life

## Saturday 12th March 2016

How many people know that today is the second Saturday in the month? If asked, who would be able to tell you when the second Tuesday is? Or the first Monday? It seems normal to me. It has become second nature to assess dinner invitations, parties, meeting around these structures. But when I step outside our church circle I realise that it is not normal. Our lives revolve around Soul Exeter (second Saturday), TEDs in homes (second Tuesday), leadership (first Monday). It can feel like an endless treadmill. Monotonous. Never-ending. Perhaps my perceptions are skewed but it can sometimes feel that every exciting invitation, every party I would like to attend, every dinner invitation falls on the second Saturday. Time and again I have to regretfully refuse invitations because we have to be at church. I don't want to resent the job, but I have to work hard not to let bitterness creep in. I love what we do and am passionately committed to it all, but I sometimes feel like I'm missing out.

## Monday 9th May 2016

The cathedral is around 900 years old and we need to be aware of that as we prepare for Upload. There are real concerns about sound levels and the strength of the roof. James is sinking under a mass of paperwork. Health and Safety assessments are not his strong point. Vision, drive, leadership and enthusiasm. These are his strengths. Admin is not. No one can help. He's got to get it done. I just try not to ask too much of him as he ploughs on with the paperwork.

## Wednesday 8th June 2016

I've never been on TV before. It is not something I have ever wanted to do, but yet again I found myself unable to say 'no' to James. I was terrified and more than a bit preoccupied with what to wear. I'm still a bit in shock that today started as any other day, but ended with me on the local news. I was displaying a magnificent cake made in the shape of Buckingham Palace as part of an article being filmed by BBC *Spotlight* on how the people of Devon and Cornwall are preparing to celebrate the Queen's ninetieth birthday. The cake was actually a weak excuse to talk about the Upload party, to put out a general invitation on TV for young people to come along and see Upload for themselves. I thought it was a brilliant idea, I just didn't want to be the person doing it. Because, in addition to feeling incredibly self-conscious, I also felt a bit of a fraud. I felt like very little of the cake was made by me. Apart from the fondant corgis (and their poo) and the fountain at the front.

It all started a couple of months ago when James had a brainwave – we could mark the fact that Upload was celebrating the Queen's birthday by giving every young person attending a piece of birthday cake. He is hoping for 2,000 young people to attend, so he needs a lot of cake, but undaunted started trying to recruit bakers. After contacting the Women's Institute, local businesses and cake shops, and receiving only a lacklustre response, he began to realise that producing 2,000 pieces of cake was going to be harder than he had anticipated. So he changed tack, turned it into a cake competition with a royal theme, and got advertising. He has worried about this competition more than perhaps anything else to do with Upload. So much so that my friend offered to make a Buckingham Palace cake for him, so that even if there were no other entries, there would be one spectacular cake. Now, I like baking cakes, but I am not a fancy cake kind of girl. The three boys in my life don't like icing so I have never had reason to even try. The few times I have made Christmas cake, it has sat in our house until July. But I offered moral support, and baked a couple of fruit cakes, and made some decorations, but the formation of the Palace was entirely down to Jo. And she was at work, so it was up to me to promote the cake and the Upload party, or our chance would be missed.

It wasn't as bad as I was expecting. I don't think I want to do it again, though. Ever.

## Saturday 11th June 2016

Today marked the end of months of preparation, and the end of a week in which it feels like we haven't seen James at all. He has had meetings at breakfast, lunch and dinner. He has come home to sleep, and that has been just about it. I'm glad it is all over. But it was worth it. Tonight was a fabulous party for young people. There was a skate park just outside the west end of the cathedral. Inside it was transformed, the side chapels full of different displays. There was a pamper zone where girls could get their nails done, or their hair curled. But more than that, it was a space where they could be listened to, be valued. There was a gaming zone. There were prayer spaces, charity displays. In the centre of the cathedral a succession of bands played. Very loudly. But the roof stayed on, thankfully. Out in the cloisters were giant inflatables. Inside and out, the cathedral was packed. We think possibly 1,500 young people came. The bishop and Mike Pilavachi talked brilliantly. My fitness tracker says I have walked ten miles, and it feels like it. The team from Unlimited have worked tirelessly for the last two days. We are all exhausted. But 1,500 young people saw God at work tonight, for them. They saw that God, and His Church, are not necessarily what they thought. It is only one step in their journey. Their journey continues from here with the friends and youth workers who brought them, who walk with them day in, day out, who know them and love them. Upload was just for one evening. But it was an unforgettable one, I think.

## Wednesday 13th July 2016

We have just been told by St Luke's school that every pupil that we have mentored either maintained their level or improved their academic performance over the year. Some have even begun to put up their hands in lessons, a mark of their increasing confidence, even if their answers aren't always the best. Before the programme started, the sad expectation was that many or all would drop even lower academically, or struggle even more with school life. I'm excited that we have been part of such a change. The whole team is encouraged before another year starts. In truth, I'm also saddened that it has actually taken very little to help these young people change the courses they were set upon. One hour, once a fortnight ... I long now to do more, for more. There are so many opportunities. We are limited only by the size of our team.

# God's Welcome

## Monday 5th September 2016

As leadership we are struggling with how we as a church should welcome visitors and new people. So far we've avoided having a welcome team, in the thought that that somehow means that those not on the team can be 'unwelcoming' that week. It seems an obvious and fundamental part of church that all of us should be welcoming. However, we've got to recognise that some people are naturals at talking to those they don't know, and some aren't. Some genuinely delight in a roomful of strangers and finding out their stories. I fear many more people are like me, where a roomful of strangers is intimidating and daunting. We are also hearing that some members of church resent the fact that they want to catch up with their friends on a Sunday, not always talk to newbies, and we want friendships to grow, to flourish. We know that some church members are struggling to feel that they fit in, that they belong. So our challenge to the church is that in every gathering we should aim to have ten minutes of uncomfortableness. Ten minutes where we step beyond ourselves, what we need or want, and look to others. We will go and make small talk to someone we don't yet know. But only for ten minutes. It is not a call to never speak to our friends. But an encouragement to always look outside ourselves.

It sounds achievable, even for me.

## Sunday 11th September 2016

Emily has come to live in our roof for a week. I think we both know that she may well end up staying in Exeter, if not our roof, for a while longer than that. I only met her a few week ago. Ours is a friendship forged at a Soul Survivor festival. I know hardly anything about her yet, but I'm looking forward to spending time with her. Currently she is between jobs, having left her last job with no clear direction as to what would come next. It seemed right to invite her to visit us. We need help this week, and she will be brilliant. But it's about more than what we need. I'm hoping that by living with our family just for a short while she will come to love our church, our city, us. I'm hoping she will want to move.

I chose to invite her to Exeter for Freshers' Week at the university. This week we run three night cafés in conjunction with the uni, the council and the police. Enthusiastic as the team are, few can cope with 12 to 3am three times in one week, and so her help will be invaluable. The fact that she is brilliant at talking to new people, at spotting those on the edge, drawing them in, loving them and valuing them, makes her an incredibly precious addition to the team.

Freshers' Week has changed beyond recognition from my day. Naïvely I remember it as a week for joining new societies, discovering where lectures and tutorials would be held, drinking many cups of coffee, and evenings spent in the bar. Either time or location has changed that, but in Exeter nowadays the week is, for many, an extravaganza of late nights, clubbing, partying and alcohol. The police, the uni, the council and ourselves all work together to keep vulnerable young people safe … New students who have set out in a strange city with a group of people they barely know, and then have drunk more than they can safely deal with, or those who have lost track of their new friends, who have no idea how to get back to the alien room in which they recently left their possessions. Time and again we meet young people struggling to keep up with their mates. Struggling to keep drinking, partying, to be appearing to have the 'time of their life'. They are shocked at the ferocity of this new life that they have entered, and are unsure in themselves and what they are doing. For some it is a terrifying week and they cannot wait for it to be over. Being situated opposite two of the nightclubs, we are uniquely placed to be a safe haven for young people like these, or for some who simply want a quiet interlude in an otherwise hectic social whirl.

## Friday 16th September 2016

James and Emily have both survived three night cafés. Both look the worse for wear. Neither has been able to sleep long into the morning. James through work commitments and Emily through an inability to stay asleep. Both have missed many precious hours of sleep this week. More than 300 students and young people came into church during the week. There were many amazing conversations and connections made. When Emily has recovered, she will drive home to Cambridge, pack up her stuff and return. My plan worked. Deep down I think we both knew it would, although we never admitted it even to ourselves. She has decided to relocate. It is brave. Another person leaving behind all that they know to come and join us in our mission. Her future is so uncertain. But I'm excited for her and for us.

## Friday 23rd September 2016

The relief of finally having a diagnosis and a way ahead is overwhelming. I have been feeling 'not right' for nearly two years. Not ill enough to stop me doing anything, but enough to make everything an effort. Enough to be tired and weary so that I question whether I want to do anything more than just what is required of me. Over a cycle of different visits to doctors there was always the sense, the hope that this time I would find out what was wrong. What could be done. Always until today those hopes were dashed, postponed until the next set of results, scans, investigations.

We've prayed for healing. Of course we have. I've asked for healing, for that miracle cure when it all seems too much to bear. And I have been healed. In part. There has been amazing restoration of both body and soul. But the problem remains. I am not alone. God is right beside me. But I'm going to have to have surgery if I want to get better.

Today with a conclusive diagnosis the way forward is clear. I will have an operation. Maybe in January. I am told it will take six weeks to recover. That seems a really long time to be sitting around feeling unwell. Or will I feel unwell? I can't imagine how I will feel. What will I do? Will I be bored? This is a trip into unknown territory. I know it is the right step.

## Saturday 24th September 2016

The relief of yesterday is over. Now I am caught up in a cycle of fear. Of worry. I remember hearing that Corrie ten Boom once described worry as 'a cycle of inefficient thought whirling around a centre of fear'.[33] It's so true. I am afraid. As much as I am relieved that the not knowing is over, I now find that I have to face some very real fears.

I find I am scared that I won't get better as quickly as they promise. That people will expect me to recover and be back and functioning before I am ready. I am scared that while I am ill I won't be there for my children. That I am letting them down. I'm scared about the unforeseen emotional and physical impact this operation might have.

These worries kept whirling through my thoughts. So I stopped. Sat with God. Examined each fear with Him, unpacked the feelings associated with each one. I was as honest as I could be and then I waited to let God speak His truth into my heart. I almost physically placed them in His hands and am now choosing to go forward knowing His peace and presence with me. I know it won't be that simple. I know the fears will come back. But I now have

---

[33] https://www.bibleinoneyear.org/bioy/commentary/2680 (accessed 19th March 2018).

eyes to spot them when they return, and I will not give in to them. I will turn back to God, and ask for His help again.

## Tuesday 4th October 2016

We started Tuesday night with a team-building game that I am not a fan of. In the game you put a sticky note on someone's back, and you all go round writing encouraging things about that person on their sticky note. Honestly, it makes me cringe inside. I can now after twenty years as a Christian pretty much predict what will be written on my note. It will say I am kind, and I am patient. And the reason it makes my toes curl is that I am not naturally either of those things. A little bit of me wants to scream out, 'If you really knew me, you wouldn't put that.' It makes me feel a little bit isolated and lonely as I think, 'You don't really know me.'

But today I wonder if I am wrong. I looked at the note and again I saw the words 'patient' and 'kind'. But this time I was struck by the fact that I have been praying for the last ten years to see the fruit of the Spirit more active in my life: 'love, joy, peace, patience, kindness, goodness, faithfulness, gentleness and self-control'.[34] I've prayed this prayer for so long because I know how lacking I am in these areas. How angry I get, how self-centred, how mean. I know I have a way to go. I always will. But I wonder today if perhaps God was showing me that the prayers are being answered. If perhaps patience and kindness are showing as fruits in my life, even when I can't see them. I know I shouldn't be surprised at this. But I am.

---

[34] Galatians 5:22-23, NIV 1984.

# Moor New Life

## Sunday 16th October 2016

Today we returned to the cottage on Dartmoor where we held our first-ever weekend away. Ten or so have stayed for the weekend; the church en masse arrived today. A church day out in a glorious setting, but with a purpose; we gathered to baptise and confirm thirteen members of our church in the stream at the foot of the hill. Forty or so members, plus the candidates' families and friends, arrived to organised chaos. The cottage that we rattled around in eight years ago was today joyously and chaotically too full. The plan had been to welcome everyone with a simple lunch of soup and bread before an afternoon of fun, culminating with the baptisms and confirmations, and then, of course, tea and cake. My simple idea of soup and bread was not so simple catering in a kitchen designed to cook for twenty, not sixty. The pans weren't big enough, the electrics fused if we ran more than one electrical item at a time. But it didn't matter. Everyone was patient. Everyone got food eventually. After lunch, people set out in their groups. Some to a wide game of 'Capture the Flag'. Here two teams each have a territory and a flag (in reality a damp tea towel) to defend. The aim of the game is to enter enemy territory and capture the flag while avoiding being captured yourself. It is a fast and furious game, made more difficult by the heather, gorse and rocks of the terrain that the teams chose to play over. Some wanted something slightly calmer, so there was also a walk, board games or just chatting by the log-burner. Everyone found something they wanted to do.

At 4pm we moved out to the river. Any residual warmth in the day had long since passed, and there was a chill in the air. I did not envy those going into the stream. Pete and James were prepared with wetsuits under their clothes. Not so the candidates. But they didn't seem to mind. Their joy in the occasion was not dampened (!) in any way. After the baptisms followed the confirmations. A simple, pared-back service led by Bishop Sarah which was made possibly even more powerful in its simplicity and the setting.

We didn't linger after the service. It was by then too cold. We jammed into the cottage to get warm, to share tea and cake and to celebrate together.

As I reflect on today, I am aware that every baptism, every confirmation service we have had in Unlimited Church has looked and felt completely different. With each bishop we have approached it in the same way. To look to use liturgy and all the wealth of the Church of England's spirituality to lead and guide what we do, while trying not to get caught up in culture or tradition 'just because'. Each service to me has been memorable and special. Each time I have seen God be present among us. Outwardly they have not looked the same. The essence of them has been identical. God's people meeting with Him in a significant way.

## Tuesday 8th November 2016

Never talk business in the bedroom. When we were newly married and James in his curacy, this was just some of the advice our vicar's wife, Daphne, shared. Over the years it has been good advice. Particularly now the children are older and seemingly always around when we might like to talk about something either private or boring (to them). It is tempting to use the privacy that comes after shutting the bedroom door to start talking. Which is a good thing, but not when it is to arrange meetings, discuss issues, share concerns. I have learned that it doesn't bother James either way. Nothing stops him sleeping. He can be asleep as soon as the conversation is finished. He can send emails in the wee small hours. He seems impervious to the hazards of both blue light and caffeine. I am not the same. I need to wind down, let the day fade away, before I can sleep. So I am the one who regularly enforces Daphne's rule. But not last night. As a leadership we meet on Monday nights – the first Monday of the month. After a full day of teaching the harp I go straight from music to dinner, to sorting out the children who will have to remain upstairs while leadership take over their living room. Josh and Toby never complain, but I'm never totally comfortable with leaving them. It's fine when they are getting on with each other and they have a shared plan for the evening. It's not easy when they are hardly talking to each other and don't want to be in the same room. However, I have no choice. Leadership will turn up at 8pm despite the mood at home. We meet from 8pm until 10pm. There is never enough time to discuss everything on the agenda. I need people to leave at 10pm so I can start winding down from the day. Even so, I am often awake at midnight and the sleep loss affects the rest of the week. James would much prefer to finish the agenda and have a late night. Even when leadership ends on time, there are often bits of the evening we want to mull over with each other. Sometimes we need to discover the other's perspective, apologise for where we were too strong, rejoice together in our church. These moments will happen in the bedroom. We break a golden rule. Business in the bedroom, but only on the first Monday of the month.

## Friday 16th December 2016

With great sadness we are stopping Night Café. It may not be a permanent decision, but appears to be what God is asking of us right now. One of the nightclubs opposite shut six months ago, and numbers at Night Café have been falling ever since. At its height, Night Café saw more than fifty visitors a night. Now the people that do come are not youth. Often they are in their twenties. Which is not old, but not the teenagers we feel called to. After a week of prayer when we specifically asked God about whether or not to continue, and opinions about what God was saying were divided, not one person came into Night Café. That has never happened before. A complete no-show. It feels like God's direction. We are surprised. The team that love Night Café, who find it edgy and exciting, are sad. We think it was a safe haven for around 1,000 young people in the wee small hours.

We wonder what is next.

## *Saturday 17th December 2016*

It still makes me smile when I refer to myself as a harpist. The very fact that I work as a musician constantly reminds me of God's sense of humour, and the fact that He does not think in any way like I do. In life, I like being in control. I like lists. I like knowing what the task is and what I need to do to achieve it. For me there is nothing better than the satisfaction of a task completed. I can't bear leaving things half-done. I am also a perfectionist. Everything needs to be done as well as I can do it. I wouldn't think twice about doing a job again if the first results were unsatisfactory or below par. None of those character traits helps me as a musician. I am constantly striving for perfection and having to be satisfied with a result that is less than perfect. I have to live with the tension of aiming for one goal, achieving another and being truly satisfied with that. Of not letting failure overwhelm me or define me. I can never tick 'harp' off any list that I might make. There is always more practice to do. It is never enough. But without it dominating my life, I have had to learn to do the best that I can do within the time that I have and to be content with what I have achieved. More than content, pleased. It has been a hard lesson, but I am learning from this that in all areas of my life I can't control everything, and everything doesn't need to be perfect.

# In Sickness and in Health

## Friday 6th January 2017

What an odd day today is going to be. I feel fine this morning. Well, not 100 per cent, but at my current level of normality. And yet I know by this evening I will be in pain, incapacitated. I'm not used to being sick. I'm not used to my body not doing exactly what I expect of it. It is a strange sense of anticipation. But as I go to hospital, I know that God is with me. I know that with the doctors I am in safe hands. I feel assured of this by the verse that I read yesterday when I was reading the Bible, 'In peace I will lie down and sleep, for you alone, Lord, make me dwell in safety.'[35] I determine to think on that verse as I wait for the anaesthetic to take effect.

---

[35] Psalm 4:8.

## Thursday 12th January 2017

For a week I have not been able to go downstairs. I am confined to my bedroom. I'm so grateful that it is a room that I love. I can only cope with a few minutes of chat before the physical effort of talking is too much for my muscles, and the mental effort of concentrating is beyond me. James has shaped his days and arranged his meetings to be around the house. I am dependent on him for every drink, everything I eat. I am not feeling well enough to want my independence back, yet. But I know I will find this dependence hard soon.

## Thursday 19th January 2017

Courgette and butternut squash. Just two of the many foods that in the last fortnight I've discovered Josh and Toby will actually eat. Who knew? We have been so looked after and loved by our church. For two weeks they have fed us every night. We've even had cake provided, as one of the things that I would do as the boys return from school is give them a piece of home-made cake. A friend knew I was worried about them missing this and so sorted out this marvellous solution. Home-made cake. Just not mine. James is finding it hard just to be grateful. It is humbling for him and makes him uncomfortable. He feels as though it is his job to provide. That he should be cooking. I see his point, but maybe what he does not see is that when he is not having to use his time in cooking he is then with Josh and Toby. He is there for the homework, for games, for chatter, where I just cannot be. By being free from cooking he can fill in my absence, which was one of my initial fears when I faced the thought of this operation. I see in this food an answer to prayer. It is way more than practical help to us. Each mouthful reminds me that we are loved, that I am not alone, that it is OK to ask for help when we are struggling. I know we could have coped without this food. I am so grateful that we did not have to.

## Friday 27th January 2017

Recovery is not a straight line. A good day is not followed by another good day. It is not like anything I have experienced before. I thought it might be like preparing for a half-marathon where it is good to push yourself to your limits to see what you can do. It isn't. Because unlike training for a marathon, when recovering from an operation if you do too much and push too hard, your body demands rest and time to heal. It does that with pain. I am learning to be gentle and patient. Not to expect too much. Not to try too hard. I have found that I cannot make this process of recovery any quicker.

## Sunday 5th February 2017

I am relieved to be back home in my bedroom again. I've spent the weekend on Dartmoor at the church weekend away. I did not really feel well enough to attend, but even worse was the thought of missing out. The reality of the weekend was much time spent in my room alone. It was good to be with everyone, but I know I was not fully present. Even small conversations exhausted me. I am glad

I went. It took more out of me than I imagined. I am looking forward to some silence.

# Classic Youth Work

*Friday 10th February 2017*

Tonight Friday Night Drop-In starts. Drop-In is for anyone from school years Nine to Thirteen from 7 to 9pm. It's advertised as a relaxed space with loads of things to do (or not do!) with games consoles, table football, table tennis, nail bar, café area with free drinks and cakes and loads more. It sounds great. It feels weird because James and I have nothing to do with it. We are here for input and advice if Pete wishes. We are praying. But this is Pete's initiative. This is what he thinks God wants. It is the first thing that has been started at Unlimited that has not required our input or us to drive it forward, to motivate, encourage and even staff it. The church is growing out from under us. It is what we have always hoped for. It is what God promised. He promised us He would build a church. That He would provide the stones. That the stones would build the church. This feels like the next stage. It is something bigger and beyond what the two of us could ever be or achieve. And it feels good.

## Thursday 16th February 2017

Recovery is lonely. I may not be alone. I have been surrounded with people, with love, with support. But that not has not prevented me from feeling lonely and despondent. Wondering if this will ever end. If I will ever feel better. Today has not been a good day. I will hope for better from tomorrow.

## Monday 6th March 2017

Back to work today. Finally, after eight weeks, not the expected six, I returned to teaching my pupils. It was hard work. I am not fully recovered. But life is returning to normal. But I find myself hoping for a new normal. Eight weeks of space and quiet have taught me so many things. I've learned how much I love people, and am so grateful for the richness that the people of church bring into our lives. It has also shown me that I need to guard and protect quiet spaces, where I can breathe and be me. I will pick up the threads of my old life, but I'm determined to use some wisdom. Not everything needs to continue as it was. Some things I did because I always have. Because it was expected of me, or because there was no one else who could. In the eight weeks I've learned I'm not indispensable, and so have other people. Now feels like a time to start afresh, to move into a new phase. To do the stuff that only I can do. The 'Liz'-shaped stuff. It is a time for running my race, the race set before me. Not anyone else's.

# Unlimited
# Celebrations

## Sunday 19th March 2017

This weekend has seen Unlimited Church celebrating our five years/ten years of existence. Ten years since James and I moved with Josh and Toby to Devon. Five years since Unlimited became a Bishop's Mission Order. On Friday night we opened up the church for a party. Inside the church was styled as a village fair with traditional stalls around the edge. The middle was space for mingling and dancing to the band. There was a hog roast. Drinks. Church was filled with people young and old. Not everyone knew what the party was about; some of our young people were not bothered in the slightest that it was celebration of what had gone before. It didn't matter. All had gathered because Unlimited was in some way important to them. Today we had a service to mark the event. The people of Unlimited gathered with the bishop, members of the council, the police, their families, their friends and other church leaders. All came to celebrate with us. Many of them had journeyed with us for part of the way.

The service looked both forward and backward. I had the joyous task of remembering all that had been. In an all too brief five minutes I got to rejoice in and retell the story of some of what God had done with us and through us. I wanted to mention everyone and everything. Every story, every stone, every person had been an important part of building the church, and I wanted my words to honour that fact, while knowing I could never achieve it. Way more would be left unsaid than said. James then got us to fix our eyes on what is ahead. We have achieved so much. Yet there is so much more to do. He called us to 'fix our eyes on Jesus, the author and perfecter of our faith' so that we can run the race set before us, throwing off 'everything that hinders and the sin that so easily entangles'.[36]

As we sat there and listened it felt in many ways as though I was hearing our vision afresh. It still feels fresh and radical rather than something I have heard many times. I know that God has more for us to do. There is more to do in the schools we are working with. The chaplaincy and mentoring roles are growing. There are more young people to meet, to get alongside. There are things we haven't even dreamt of yet. We heard this week that the long-term rental agreement is finally in place – the building project can recommence. I'm excited for the journey to come. I thought I knew these verses; we have studied, lived and prayed these first two verses from Hebrews 12 for ten years. But today I was struck anew by the end of the verse

---

[36] Hebrews 12:1-2, NIV 1984.

that follows them. We are called to look to Jesus 'so that you will not grow weary and lose heart'.[37] I know in our journey to this point I have often been weary. I have often lost heart. But God also knows that. It was not even unexpected to Him. He knew I would struggle. He knows we will all struggle. That we will face opposition, both from the outside and from within ourselves. And through it all He gently points us to fix our eyes on Jesus, who begins it all, perfects it all, understands us all.

God knows me. He knows my weaknesses and my strengths. He loves me just the way I am. He is enough for me.

---

[37] Hebrews 12:3.

# Acknowledgements

My thanks must go to the very many people who have been part of Unlimited or who have supported us over the years. I cannot express how grateful I am for all the love and support you have shown us in so many ways. Many of whom are named here:

*Chris Ablett, Dave Ablett, Bruce Anderson, Naomi Armstrong, Bishop Robert Atwell, Joshua Bailey-Brown, Charis Baker, David Baker, Eve Balshaw, Naomi Bament, Dave Barlow, Georgia Battye, Richard Bellamy, Jasmine Bennett, Wade Berry, Josh Bessant, Jess Best, Joe Bint, Dom Borg, Cam Boyle, Hannah Brewer, Anna Broadbent, Heidi Budden, Hannah Burden, Saskia Butler, Jenny Butt, Sarah Camp, Ben Chadwick, Tim Chamings, Andrew Chapman, Emily Charkham, Tim Chau, Naa Chinery-Hesse, Sophie Clowrey, Olivia Colbeck, Tom Collins, Heather Courtney, Elly Crook, Chris Cross, Evan Davy, Ellie Dawson, Emily Dixon, Charlotte Draper, Penny Driver, Lauren Dudley-Clarke, Barry Dugmore, Eley Dyson, Steve Dyson, Norvie Dzimega, Amy Elliott, Jack England, Charlie Evans, Adam Eveleigh, Bishop Bob Evens, Katie Farrell, Chris Ferrier,*

*Madeleine Fischer, Martin Follett, Amanda Ford, Sophie Ford, Eleanor Fox, Lizzie Frost, Rachel Frost, Christopher Futcher, Alice Gausden, Nikita Gill, Sam Glazebrook, Toby Glazebrook, Jenna Gordon, Katy Gosling, Annabel Goulding, Abigail Grant, Josh Grier, Toby Grier, Sara Grier, Alex Griffiths, Zerelda Hamilton, Marina Hannus, Chris Hansford, Sarah Hansford, Chris Harris, Laura Harris, Sophie Harry, Isabelle Hawksworth, Meg Hobbs, Ed Hodges, Jess Hodges, Connor Howe, Emma Hughes, Dan James, Ollie James, Annie Jeffries, Ed Johnson, Megan Jones-Dellaportas, Amie Keeling, Tehila-Joy Keeling, Shah Kellman, Lily Kerfoot, Angie Kerslake, Jack Kerslake, Marc Kerslake, Tim Kimber, Aaron Kimber, James Kimber, Judith Kimber, Jo Kirkcaldy, Daniel Kitchener, Josh Knight, Simon Lane, Bishop Michael Langrish, Dan Lawther, Rachel Leeson, Cheyenne Lepird, Theres Lessing, Anna Liechtenstein, Charlie Littlewood, Pippa Loescher, Bryony Loveless, Sarah Marks, Kyle McKay, Bishop Nick McKinnel, Tamsin McLeod, Ella Morris, Ruth Morris, Bishop Sarah Mullally, Tom Murray, Hannah New, Bekah Norman-Walker, Anna Norman-Walker, Pete Norris, Rachel Norris, Seun Olusanya, Carolyn Orchard, Henry Ormerod, Samantha Over, Rachel Partridge, Mike Partridge, Will Partridge, Hannah Peck, Olly Pendry, Steve Pollard, Helen Pollard, Sam Pollard, Anna Pollard, Tilly Porthouse, Cesca Priestley, Natalie Pursglove, Georgie Reay, Paul Reisbach, Sian Rice, Catherine Rossiter, Suzy Rushforth, James Rushforth, Mark Rylands, April Sargeant, Hannah Schirrmacher, Jenny Sexton, Amelie Sievers, Gemma Simpson, Tom Simpson, Jo Soper, Jon Soper, Ellie Sperling, Tom Squance, Trina Squance, Paul Squance, Esther Squance, Kate Stone, Josh Stribling, Philip Sourbut, Andrew Southall, Averil Swanton, Sheila Swarbrick, Justine Tear, Martin Thompson, Stacey Towell, Daisie Tranah,*

*Wes Tyrell, Jen van den Berg, Joe Wait, Jack Wakefield, Keith Walton, Lissy Webb, James West, Ruth West, Guy West, Tania West, Luke While, Ben Wilkins, Harry Wilmot, Ant Wilson, Tatty Wilson, Caitlin Woodman, Lizzie Woolls, Amelia Woolway, Beth Wragg, Alison Young*

This book would not be complete without at least a nod to the literally hundreds of wonderful young people that we have met. I have been heartened by our conversations. Amazed that you accepted rather than rejected us. From the beginning we tried to record your names. We haven't been entirely successful. Where some names have come up many times over the years, I have recorded them only once. Others are quite unique!

*Abby, Adam, Aiden, Al, Alice, Alisha, Allie, Amber, Amelia, Amy, Ana, Angus, Anna, Annie, Archie, Arthur, Asha, Ayesha, Aziz, Ben, Beth, Bethany, Billy, Bluebell, Bobby, Bonnie, Brianna, Bruce, Caleb, Callum, Cam, Cameron, Cara, Caroline, Caspian, Cassady, Ceris, Chantelle, Charlie, Charlotte, Chelsea, Cher, Chloe, Chris, Cian, Clara, Cohen, Conner, Connor, Coray, Crystal, Daisy, Damo, Dayanta, Dean, Derek, Django, Dot, Eboni, Edward, Eli, Ella, Elle, Ellis, Eloisa, Emily, Enna, Esben, Esme, Esmee, Felix, Finlay, Finn, Flo, Fran, Frank, Frank, Freya, Gabriel, Gemma, Georgia, Gerald, Giselle, Govinda, Grace, Greg, Harley, Harriet, Harry, Hattie, Haya, Heather, Henry, Hiba, Holly, Hugh, Indi, Iona, Isaac, Issy, Izzy, Jacob, Jadine, Jake, Jake, Jakob, James, Jasmine, Jay, JD, Jemima, Jess, Jo, Jodie, Joe, Joël, Joelle, Jordan, Jordanna, Josh, Justine, Kai, Kane, Kate, Kathryn, Katie, Katja, Katy, Kayleigh, Kieran, Kitty, Kwasi, Kyran, Leah, Leigh-Ann, Leo, Les, Liam, Liezel, Lillie, Lizzie,*

*Lottie, Lou, Louis, Lucas, Lucy, Luke, Lydia, Maisey, Makayla, Malcolm, Mark, Martha, Matilda, Matt, Maya, Megan, Meggan, Mercy, Mia, Misra, Molly, Nadine, Nathan, Niall, Niamh, Noah, Nora, Olive, Olivia, Paige, Phoebe, Phoenix, Pippa, Rachel, Reanna, Rhia, Rhiannon, Rich, Robin, Romany, Romi, Rosa, Rosie, Ross, Rowan, Ruairi, Ruby, Sally, Sam, Sammi, Sammy, Sarah, Scarlett, Seth, Shannon, Shelbie, Shenda, Sian, Sian, Siobhan, Sol, Solomon, Sophia, Sophie, Sorya, Stan, Stephen, Stewart, Stu, Tam, Tamsin, Tamzy, Tara, Teaghan, Tia, Tiffany, Tim, Toby, Tom, Toni, Tristan, Verity, Vicky, Wez, Will, Willow, Wolly, Yasmin, Zach, Zany*

And finally I must offer my huge thanks to all at Instant Apostle for believing in this book and making it happen. You are an incredible team and it has been a privilege to work with you.